Contents

Dam-Burst of Dreams

Dam-Burst of Dreams is a collection of the unique writings of Christy Nolan, now fifteen, who has never been able to speak or totally control his movements. His remarkable talent was only released four years ago when he was introduced to a muscular-relaxant drug which has given him sufficient control to compose, first with the aid of an electric typewriter and now with a word-processor, manipulated by a 'unicorn' stick attached to his head. This volume consists of his verse, short stories and plays, including the autobiography, 'A Mammy Encomium', for which he won the British Spastics Society 1979 literary award.

Dam-Burst of Dreams

The Writings of
CHRISTOPHER NOLAN

Introduction by
Marjorie Wallace

Pan Books
London, Sydney and Auckland

First published in Great Britain 1981 by
George Weidenfeld and Nicholson Ltd
This edition published 1988 by Pan Books Ltd,
Cavaye Place, London SW10 9PG
9 8 7 6 5 4 3 2
© Christopher Nolan 1981
Introduction © Marjorie Wallace 1981
ISBN 0 330 30317 1
Printed and bound in Great Britain by
Richard Clay Ltd, Bungay, Suffolk

Introduction

Christopher Nolan was eleven years old before anyone knew he
could write. He would sit, propped in his wheelchair, staring at
the grey Dublin skies, while he listened to the voices of his family
and their friends, able to take part only through the unique
communication he has evolved with his mother and the fierce
intelligence of his blue eyes. Today, four years later, he is a poet
of merit, of extraordinary maturity, as steeped in Irishness as
Seamus Heaney, and true to the tradition of rich imagery and
sonorous phrases as Yeats or Joyce.

Christopher's handicap was caused by a difficult birth that dis-
rupted the motor centres of his brain, leaving his body an in-
complete jigsaw, with useless limbs, uncoordinated movements
and a voice that is generally incoherent. But his mind was left
unimpaired and the sharpness and power of his perception
impeccable. Christopher Nolan grew up a hostage to his own
body, gazing out through the crystal window of his eyes, a specta-
tor before the world, yet unable to respond, to comment, to reply.
Image upon image ricocheted round his skull and burned into
his consciousness. Without means of expression, the pressure to
communicate was intolerable.

In his eleventh year his life was transformed by a drug, Lio-
resal, which relaxed the muscles of his neck sufficiently to allow
him partial control of his head for short periods of time. It was
a minor pharmacological victory, but for Christopher that min-
imal command opened a wide doorway of communication. The
clinic he attended made him a 'unicorn' stick to fit on his fore-
head, and with a little support for his head, he learned how to
type by pointing the unicorn on to the keys of the typewriter.
Encouraged, the Nolans bought an electric typewriter, and Ber-
nadette, with a steadying hand cupped under Christopher's chin,
helped him to compose a thank-you letter to an aunt. Unsteadily,
Christopher struggled to reach the keys, to line his unicorn up
to the one he wanted and, by nodding his head, to depress it. All
his concentration was needed to type each letter. Then, suddenly,

the unsteady head in Bernadette's hand revealed a will of its own as Christopher reached for letters of his own choice.

'Until then we had no idea whether he could write or spell nor that he knew such long words,' says Kathleen Ryan, head teacher at his remedial school. 'We knew he could read, but that was very limited because someone had to be with him to turn the pages. I admit we were surprised by the strange language.'

His mind unlocked, Christopher, partnered by his mother, tapped out his first poem, 'I Learn to Bow', full of the alliteration which characterizes much of his work.

Within two days he had written a second poem, 'I Peer Through Ugliness', giving more insight into his secret world. 'So you've been writing these poems in your head all this time?' Bernadette asked him. Christopher rolled his eyes upwards to say 'Yes'.

'My Ambitions', written just a month later, gave the first hint of the epigrammatic style he later developed in his prose and contained a touching reference to the drug which had given him his outlet:

> Taste of pity as people stare,
> Love, lots of love from mother,
> Pills you find as lasting prayer,
> An irate person may possibly
> Have faith, instead of despair.

Christopher was born at County Hospital, Mullingar on 6 September 1965. His father, Joseph Nolan, owned a farm, but was by profession a psychiatric nurse at the mental hospital nearby. His mother, Bernadette, had been a book-keeper before she married. His sister, Yvonne, was then just two years old. The birth was a difficult one and eventually the baby was delivered by caesarian section. It soon became clear that Christopher had been severely brain-damaged as a result of asphyxiation.

As the child grew up, Bernadette recognized his intelligence, perception and wit. Gradually the whole family learned they could communicate with Christopher through his eyes. 'I was teaching him all the time,' says Bernadette Nolan. 'We had letters of the alphabet all round the walls of the kitchen and each letter was illustrated by one of my own drawings. He learned how to spell words by accumulating groups of letters. He used his eyes to indicate which letter came next in the word which he was attempting to spell. He memorized the look of each word and was always fascinated by the rich sound of unusual words.'

The first breakthrough for Christopher came when the Nolans met Dr Ciaran Barry, medical director of the Central Remedial Clinic in Dublin. Dr Barry accepted without question Bernadette's belief that her son was an intelligent child isolated only by his inability to communicate. 'What are you going to do about his education?' he asked. He suggested Christopher should go to Dublin to the school attached to the Clinic. The Nolans eventually found a house a few doors away and on 7 January 1973 Christopher enrolled at his new school.

There the teachers, occupational therapists and doctors tried to find ways of prising out his trapped intelligence. Bernadette's belief that he was very bright was vindicated. On two occasions a psychologist assessed his IQ as being five years above the average for his age. But it was not until the Clinic made it possible for him to type that his skill with words was apparent.

How has such a handicapped child acquired his extraordinary style and vocabulary? 'It is as though he has been playing with words all his childhood as other, able-bodied, children play with toys', Bernadette explains. He seems to cherish them, to savour their sound, to explore their meaning, to place them in relation to one another like friends round a dinner table. It is not simply the span of vocabulary Christopher uses, but the accuracy and economy with which he targets his words, that is unnerving. 'A Mammy Encomium' is the title of his autobiography. Where did he find that archaic but wholly appropriate 'encomium' (a eulogy, high-flown formal praise) without being widely read, or even being able to reach for a dictionary? In the poem 'Snowflakes', he uses the description 'A god in mephitis'. We turn apprehensively to the dictionary (Mephitis: noxious or pestilential emanation, especially from the earth) and shudder at the sharpness of its use. He even weaves classical allusions into his

verse: Nemesis, the goddess of retribution, and cestus, Andro-
meda's love-lustre girdle.

But the real mystery of Christopher's writing lies deeper than
vocabulary: it is in the smouldering, tense, archetypal images
with which he fills his pages. They reach up from his subcon-
scious, uncanny, exotic, in turn threatening, doom-laden and
hopeful. The air of mystery, the echo of witchcraft and black
magic are accentuated by his choice of names for his characters.
Merimba Perangamo is the guilt-ridden anti-hero of his first
prose work, who kills Ruth Eshuba's parents in a dare-devil
driving stunt, and only gains her as his wife after she, too, has
been paralysed by a car crash.

In 'Perangamo' Christopher writes:

> No peace could erase Merimba's mounting leopard-spot-
> ted damnation, he all anxiously appeared to Ruth at the
> cemetery and gabbled greedily, into lonely moribund all lost
> eyes. All Merimba moaned about, Ruth amounted a passing
> summary dumb silence, she feared feelings of doom and
> moaning all mournfully she groped her way from the
> cemetery.

'He animates dead metaphors and expressions in a startling
way', says Christopher Ricks, Professor of English at Cambridge
University. 'The landscape is grim and dead, his characters are
frozen into postures as in a Beckett play, but the language is
young and energetic. He uses words as though he were passing
electric shocks through a dead body. Old clichés and disused
words are brought horrifyingly to life by the sinister and the
supernatural.'

The Frankenstein image explains a lot about Christopher. His
written words are his only means of 'zombieing' paralysed limbs
and encumbering body into life. They are his personality, his
totality. The glimpse we see into his encapsulated mind is un-
conventional, because Christopher has never had the opportun-
ity to learn conventions. It is surrealistic because his perception
of the world is not palpable. He belongs to this world, but is not
part of it. He is suspended between life and death, continually

in conflict: a conflict which is echoed in all his images. 'A god in mephitis': the delicate white snow conceals the noxious emanation, but the conflict is unresolved and the threat remains.

Continually we are reminded of the interplay of opposites, of hope and despair, pleasure and sadness, pain and joy. In his play 'Nobody' (where stage instructions and dialogue complement each other in dynamic counterpoint) Christopher Ball, 'a weasel-sad, lost ex-priest', explains: 'Nobody ever knows feelings of pain without loitering sometimes in the realms of apparent azure blue aloe happiness.' Note the interplay of the hopeful words 'azure blue' and 'happiness' with the bitter 'aloe' and disbelieving 'apparent'. The play is set in Dingle, a beautiful County Kerry fishing village. But even in his description the conflict remains: 'Tokens of joisting summer breezes mingle mournfully, spooning pleasure into the Dingle Peninsula.' Similarly, when he describes his grandparents as 'Aged sentinels, sampling Death's éclat' we are struck again by the juxtaposition of ideas – expecting a downbeat word we are suddenly uplifted by the exuberance of 'éclat'.

Christopher displays the processes within his mind in the poem 'Could You?':

> . . . My harried brain leaned
> Downward on my chest, thinking, memorizing,
> Repeating, listening in my ear for the
> Effect of my words. I realized my munificence
> Of knowledge. I endangered my freedom
> Of expression, if I did not disembowel
> My notorious madness, in impeccable
> Language, agonizingly written, in numerous
> Tantalizing, spasmodic-ridden onslaughts,
> On a rickety, moaning typewriter

With no voice of his own, it would be interesting to know whose voice he hears pounding out the melodic lines. For Christopher's writing is full of euphony. On those rare occasions when vocabularly fails him, he does not hesitate to make up words that may be etymologically eccentric, but fit his pattern of sound. For instance, in his poem 'Death', he writes of 'peace' as:

> A treasure only surely sapespered
> During the dolorous days of death.

'Sapespered' is a Nolan-built portmanteau, combining the Latin roots meaning taste and hope.

In his 'Mammy Encomium', he described his own birth: 'Nora Meehan brought one baby onto the earth under normal circumstances, she now was labouring to give birth to her gelatinous, moaning, dankerous baby boy.' 'Dankerous' is a made-up word, its roots are obvious and evocative, but it is for its sound that it has been primarily selected.

Christopher Nolan's image-intoxicated poems have something in common with those of Gerard Manley Hopkins, the only poet with whose works he has begun to be familiar. (Christopher does not often like having poetry read to him. He prefers to keep his mind unconditioned and develop his own ideas.) Like Hopkins', his works are indigestibly rich on first acquaintance. The reader is assailed with a cacophony laced with the dissonances of contrast and conflict. The scale is universal, heroic, like a Wagner opera, then suddenly taut, intimate and simple.

Like Hopkins, Christopher has picked up the strange words which form his musical notation as gleanings of conversations overheard, snatches of Gaelic, doctors' whispered consultations. And from these elements, blended with items from radio and television, he creates his own conglomerate vocabulary.

Hopkins' best work was probably that of his last period when he was teaching in University College, Dublin, unhappy and frustrated by ill-health. 'In that coffin of weakness and dejection in which I live', he wrote, his weak body was unable to keep pace with the urgency of his mind. For Christopher, that problem has been extreme for his near total handicap has given him only a brain to exercise. 'Vulnerably,' he writes, 'he ceased asking some drowsy limbs to fear putridly negative pursuits and germinated hundreds, perhaps millions of idle brain cells instead.' Thus, as blind people develop their sense of hearing to compensate for their dead eyes, Christopher has compensated for his useless body by using his mind. His handicap is his advantage. The use of his mind is his life, his work, his hobby, his engrossment. Our distractions and temptations mean nothing to him.

It is when a poem is completed in his mind that handicap's advantage becomes a cruel barrier. His words must be squeezed through the unicorn onto his typewriter. At first every word was a 10 to 15 minute battle. The 2000 word prose-poem 'Perangamo' took 50 hours over 24 days to complete. The sheer labour of typing has had its effects on Christopher's work, by creating a discipline in which every word must play many parts, through its meanings, the evocation of its sound, its shape and rhythm and, most important, its relationship to its neighbours. The result is a dazzling explosion of words, extraordinarily dense in texture, like a heavily orchestrated score, whose subtlety and skill only become apparent after many hearings.

Christopher's success in communicating such richness through so thin a thread is due largely to his mother, his patient amanuensis. She steadies his head to make typing possible, checks unusual spellings in the dictionary for him and struggles to understand what he wants. Because he picks up most words by sound alone, Christopher finds difficulty in spelling them and the occasional idiosyncrasies of his spelling and punctuation are retained in the pieces as they appear here. In his poem 'Dastardly he wanted to use the word 'masochistic', whose meaning he knew, but which he had not heard distinctly. At first he wrote 'masokiz' but Bernadette was unable to interpret it. After many attempts he became frustrated and substituted 'cowardly'. Ten days later he managed to discover the correct spelling and the word was replaced.

Christopher Nolan's work first came to light when he won a literary competition run by the Spastics' Society. Subsequently, I told his story and reproduced some of his poems in *The Sunday Times Magazine*. Following the article, Phil Odor, a computer scientist from Edinburgh University, suggested a micro-computer could be used to help Christopher communicate more readily and, in particular, to speed-up his typing. *The Sunday Times*

xiv   *Introduction*

appealed to its readers for £2,200 to buy Christopher's computer.
There were more than 2000 replies from all parts of the world
enclosing cheques and offers of help amounting to over £40,000.

The machine is changing Christopher's life by giving him
much greater independence. Apart from learning to write with
it, he is able to use the computer to play games for the first time
and to control the radio and television himself. The money
which was contributed to help him has been placed at his request
in a charitable Trust to aid other similarly disabled children, to
which part of the proceeds of this book are being donated.

In his latest works Christopher concentrates on expressing his
own developing philosophy: his coming to terms with the disap-
pointment of his body and the demands of his talent. In parti-
cular, the poetic sequence 'Lovely Months' counterpoints his
struggle between mind and body. It consists of twelve poems,
one for each month of the year, but also, cleverly representing
the first twelve years of his life. The stark 'January' deals with
his birth, his near death and his escape to brain-damaged sur-
vival:

> Changing moribund mourning to numbness.

'February' is a period of confusion, conflict, anger and amor-
phous hopelessness. By 'March' some order is appearing. In
'April' he has become aware of himself and the world's view of
him:

> Classed mammy-dallied appointed April-Fool.

In 'May' he recognizes the strength and devotion of his mother,
a theme which is extended in 'June' to embrace the whole family
held together by his parents' marriage vows; in 'July' he asserts
himself against Life's bullies, supported by 'numerous knights,/
Beating naughty moots mutations'.

In 'August' his school life begins and his rising hope of the
summer months is confirmed:

> Schooling lets merit spring-step straight
> Towards seeming brilliant careers, mastering

> Centuries non-ligamented, muchly-longed lease,
> Changing much cental, cubbyholed secrets. . . .

In 'September' he is beginning to live and by 'October', the most beautiful and moving of the poems, there is fruitfulness, serenity, a coming to terms, but still conflict. He describes the 'oven-like nuts' as:

> centuries
> Coined, small kernel-assimilations,
> Cement-hard shells cream-tipping life. . . .

In the 'November' month, just as nature needs to slumber, so too must Christopher, seeming asleep, keep an ever-alert ear. In 'zany, bonny December' he has finally learned to accept the dichotomous world in which he lives.

The same philosophy permeates his latest play 'Nobody', but with the added realization that he can now speak for the speechless, like himself, who still cannot be heard. His writings overflow with the message that only by accepting the suffering of disadvantage can you transcend it. 'Nobody nurses grief kindly,' says one of the characters in the play, 'but man wins when he does.'

Marjorie Wallace

Writings

Age 11–12 Years

'I have been mentally writing poetry since I was three years old', Christy told me one day. That revelation set me thinking and indeed made sense as my mind flashed back over the years, remembering all of the times my gaze fell upon him as he sat in a small wooden chair, his head tilted to one side whilst upon his face lingered an expression of deep concentration. A sudden question from me always seemed to startle him as he struggled to return to the ordinary world.

Nowadays I oftentimes sit and talk with him about his early years of silent repression. He comforts my disquietude by laughingly pointing out that his mind had never been idle. He spent his long days composing poetry, learning it by heart and then storing it away in individual compartments in his mind, whilst at the same time praying that some day, somehow, he would find the means to express those poems in written words.

That long-awaited day came on 20 August 1977. Thus, all of the writings in this section must be seen in the light of prose and poetry which he had already worked upon.

Bernadette Nolan

A Mammy Encomium

Mosaim Poaberry baned much moans muttered by his patient
Mrs. Nora Meehan. Much moans now and then locked pale
Nora Meehan in man-paralysing agony. Mosaim felt dread
mounting in his Persian, baned, beautiful heart. Mosaim
Poaberry arrived in Mullingar to reside at The County Hospital,
bringing with him all the medical memorabilia and skills
developed from long, lamentably lonely periods as a medical
doctor in Persia.

Nora Meehan brought one baby onto the earth under normal
circumstances, she now was labouring to give birth to her
gelatinous, moaning, dankerous baby boy. Mosaim Poaberry's
X-rays on Nora Meehan indicated baby not moving normally,
making a comaical, moaning Mrs. Nora Meehan casualty victim
needing immediate, bloody Caesarean Surgery.

Mosaim Poaberry salved all hope, Baby Meehan might just
survive. Fists clenched, hearing not functioning, breathing ulti-
mately, loss appearing on heart pulse, sapidity placing fresh
formsuds one move nearer in yelling Baby Meehan.

Mussa Molahg moved Baby Meehan's lace mantle and en-
closed a cellular capsule to measure Baby Meehan's respiration.
Mrs. Nora Meehan pleaded mightily, coldly moaning for
her son. Accounts from the Dublin Hospital to which Baby
Meehan had been urgently dispatched allowed some hope to
dearly dwell in Meehan parent hearts. Mussa Molahg looked
pure Indian and truly he was. Mussa came to Dublin to study
medicine, meaning to return to his native Bombay on completing
his lot of ponderous training. Mussa came to the conclusion that
Baby Meehan might by the negative response he noticed be
minus his hearing. He set out magically to rectify the ear orifice,
nothing very serious manifested itself.

Mosaim Poaberry meanwhile positively prepared Nora Mee-
han for another operation, fleetingly he glanced at her tummy

and mightily prayed the man wielding the knife an easy balanced
hand. Most times caring associations meet anxious dads follow-
ing difficult, delicate births, Matthew Meehan bore poor sadness
more manfully than most. Matthew calmly, malevolently,
passionately succumbed to anaesthetising himself coldly with
motivating all potent, electric meteors of God-unifying lovely
prayer.

Nora Meehan mowed the lawn all green, using all help laugh-
ingly, lovingly given by her daughter Yvonne. Mr. Matthew
Meehan nominated much zealous, noble names acclaiming god-
liness, not following the current trend of Meehan names he
suggested sad, simple Joseph.

Mrs. Nora Meehan used lots of poor, pondering, perplexing
pommeling, moving Joseph's legs and arms manually, gearing
negative brain-damaged, paralysed limbs into locking wonky
order. Most microplasmic molecule matter moltifies, moaning
all miserably, obdurately into lives, but poor Joseph Meehan
most mercilessly boycotted of the Dublin Hospital medical aid at
birth, tore at bold life with no heed sometimes for his poor
handicapped limbs.

Although everyone thought that Joseph Meehan might be
passing swiftly from this life, dolefully he sagaciously held on.
Vulnerably he ceased asking some drowsy limbs to fear putridly
negative pursuits and germinated hundreds, perhaps millions of
idle brain cells instead.

Not mobile meant Joseph painfully made mundane plans,
looking manfully, poorly, longingly for desirable, foolish, much
ameliorated, natural putrid order. Matthew Meehan mourned
love's misuse of fruitfull limbs and giving much mulling, boldly
buttressed buttocks worn boldly lean and shell-like. Nora Mee-
han mellifluously moulded muscles meant to maelstrom severely.
Petals practically pistiled lean pollen bowls, all knells moaned
Baby Meehan's plight.

Nearly all monstrous beauties burst mesmerizingly on Joseph
Meehan's chest, most events posterity preambles upon, but the
lease of desirable force, powering loads ponderously moving
teeming ideas, merits glorious, mind-boggling time.

Mrs. Nora Meehan loudly called for her husband and said "Matthew, more manly effort wants to be a great goal leaning powerfully in the direction of Joseph's malady". Matthew Meehan mollified his wife moodily mournfully manfully, comically always looking at God-embroidered smog masterfully.

Mould lulls man into waning. Games made Joseph look horribly comatose. Among many good friends he counted lovely lonely Nora Meehan as cement, cementing calm moulding nonchalantly around lost, sorrowful, lifeless limbs.

Molars developed in Joseph Meehan's mouth, molars appearing in a mouth which was never to know the moist mincing milky awareness of food being masticated. Money meant very little to Joseph's poor patient parents, past experience appeared of passing faintly-little amelioration. Lots of people puzzled anxiously, annoyingly among themselves, wanting a boy appearing lancinated all ambiently, to amass all ambitions, accomplishments and appearances Apollo-pandering mothers mulishly longed.

Manly Matthew Meehan maddened his team's villainous John McEvoy in football by temperate peaceable playing. Peace mellowed many of heaven's holy, heavy, hungry, painful babyhood, day-long dreams for Joseph Meehan. Peace dimmed Matthew's ambitions and Joseph's gaping, gangling appearance managed to be beautifully bearable.

A Morris Minor car always came in useful for Joseph Meehan's family. In fumes issuing uncontrollably inside the car, uncrying in motion, tame Nora Meehan managed to bottle Joseph's milk awkwardly, slowly down Joseph's throat.

Mrs. Nora Meehan met Dr. Maureen Mooney, medical doctor living in Dublin and she discussed Joseph's constant crying thoroughly, yearning longingly for possible panacea – lovely lasting lamb minced in a 'Mouli' mincer and Dr. Mooney became her holy hero. A melon-coloured cooker cooked lovely meaty succulent stews for Joseph Meehan making Matthew, Nora and Yvonne applaud, knowing they would watch Joseph sleep contentedly all night.

Grandad John Power dressed himself that morning and

shaved, knowing he did so for the very last time. A man omitting nothing meritorious in this fortitudeness life, he faced his God all glorious without a worry. Matthew moved Grandad Power, pounding his chest anxiously as the ailing heart spluttered to a moan. Moan met moan as Nora Meehan lifted Joseph in her arms and giving Yvonne her hand led her from fear.

Mrs. Nora Meehan, a pan always kept especially for heating nourishing creamy milk, allowed Joseph's breakfast to cool before spoon-feeding claret-coloured tonic Incremin and painstakingly dosing the baby.

A pilgrimage to Lourdes most holy mentioned Matthew and Joseph Meehan on its featured form of departure. Matthew clearly exposed patient pangs of panic paralysing nature. Joseph, always nervous of failing to fly, knowing his balance took toll of his tummy, annoyed his father by crying worryingly on the pilgrimage.

Dr. Ciaran Barry smiled encouragingly, calming Nora's meek, mild molestations. Nora Meehan and Joseph met the man who was to be Joseph's doctor all metacentre and he mentioned The C.R.C. School to Mrs. Meehan. Appointment followed appointment and where Joseph was concerned, much mulling, long planning and loving minding, managed arable land to make, from arid, dry desert.

Central Remedial Clinic School enrolled Joseph Meehan as a pupil on 7th January 1973. All Mullingar schools catered for normal, ablebodied children, but Joseph mattered little to schools such as these; most matters of Joseph's education meant lots of hardship to all the rest of the family. Matthew Meehan moved from Mullingar Psychiatric Hospital where he was employed as a Male Nurse. Leaving cost moments of doubt as it meant losing all his seniority. Matthew had to consider too vacating his peaceful, bold farm and all his cattle, sheep and Yvonne's dappled-grey Connemara Pony.

Yvonne Meehan appeared happy enough in her new school, an enormous school compared to her old one in the nearby village where she loved loyal friends. Yvonne who more than anyone else gave encouragement to Joseph came to Dublin leaving a class of eight to join one of forty-three pupils in her new school.

Nora Meehan now made everything pass off normally, time meant nothing to her as every possible allowance was made – action encouraged Matthew Meehan and Nora, Yvonne and Joseph. All Matthew's mocking mates waylaid him with mullings of taboo.

Grannie Mary Ann Meehan talked magically, dimly of her husband, sad expressions hovered over her handsome face as she remembered Joseph. Mary Ann Meehan remembered Matthew and his father making hay in the meadowfield beside the house as she set off for school in peaceful Fore Village. Nora Meehan listened intently as the old woman slowly unfolded the iconography of Glenidan. Mary Ann told Nora of years which she spent teaching children reading, writing and arithmatic. Nora smiled mischievously as Mary Ann told of Joseph's love of writing. "Oftentimes" the old woman went on "I remember coming home from school in the late evening to find the patient horses attached to the plough while Joseph who had sudden inspiration, sat idle, writing his endless poetry and prose".

Matthew Meehan poured out his tea very slowly, making sure not to cry, putting on a brave face in front of his children. Moaning quietly he grabbed a bite to eat before moving to close all windows. An urgent phonecall had brought the mournful news, Grannie Meehan had gone to heaven, to Joseph, who had already gone to meet his Maker.

Peace moves in lovely ways. Nora Meehan managed to make life interesting, lively and gay for all her family. Many lovely sunny days saw poor amiable Nora pack fresh sandwiches, fill a basket full of all types of goodies and setting off for a beautiful day in the great valleys among the Dublin Mountains

Nora Meehan locked poor Bruce in his kennel before retiring for the night. Bruce was a big black and white Collie Dog which Matthew more or less depended upon to help him round up his cattle and sheep on the farm. Rapid changes lessened Bruce's usefulness, he now lay around in his new gay home in Dublin.

almost always panting excitedly as Joseph arrived home from school.

Matthew Meehan moved topaz-coloured material from inside a carton and revealed a mossgreen bottle of lovely nourishing wine. Nora made everybody seem sullen as she naturally made all fiscal arrangements around the family finances. Nora made noises of excitement and pleasure as a lovely dinner party was planned. She announced a party in honour of Matthew's birthday which was coming very soon.

Matthew made every effort to effectively ease Nora's painful piteous plight. He made allowances all peaceful, all patient, all meticulous as Joseph moved locked, lost limbs in involuntary movements. Joseph always carped, always appealing for time to tackle tame and timid efforts to eat. Eating, poor Joseph possibly found, took toll of everyone's patience. Talking to Joseph as he struggled, loathing all his ghastly attempts to master the sad martyrdom of his spasms helped to allay the fallow feeling of food being rejected by his stomach.

Joseph Meehan nominated all classmates in school. All pupils seemed anxious to solve his loneliness. Mrs. Lennon appealed to Malachy, "sit beside Joseph and let him look at your book", as an old boy, Malachy learned before all about lovely dreams being sadly shattered on starting school. Malachy Moran helped Joseph to minimize many tasks of school-life which sincerely bothered him. Mrs. Byrne helped Joseph call a stop to his crying, using an old duster called experience, she calmed his sad sobs . . . Dapper domes detract dreams all drizzling, somehow.

Matthew Meehan allowed Yvonne a solitary nostalgic sail – massing many memories of Milltownpass, appeasement set-in, dispelling masterfully all Yvonne's miserable feelings and demands to escape back to the farm.

Malachy Moran always attempted to assist Joseph Meehan. Nora lovingly left Joseph at school each morning to be slowly wheeled into his classroom for roll-call at 9.30. Mrs. Gallagher taught Joseph during his second year in school. During class time Joseph sat idling. Malachy needed Joseph and Joseph needed Malachy, all messages to the teacher went via Malachy.

School became boring now for Joseph. Nora thanked Mrs. Byrne, the principal, for basting Joseph's timid, brain-damaged stacking of high, book-fresh ideas, when she changed him to third class.

Steel-like, Joseph continued all timidly, all sullenly, all masterfully to struggle against his horrid handicap. Nora worked mightily to help Joseph to brink book-strewn channels to knowledge. A strike slows teacher's offer, sending lots of happy, halcyon children home to carry-on.

Joseph's ambition longingly strayed towards writing, so a long, tiring, tame training took trembling years to learn. Nora moved Yvonne's card of mending thread leaving alot of handmade clothes to be mended. Too many chores irked calm, cool Nora. Last minute manoeuvring always allowed Nora's intolerance-allowance altimeter to hover docile.

Matthew Meehan moreover allowed smiles to creep busily across his kindly face. Calamity nolonger solely schooled, nulling Matthew's assets, letting Joseph learn all there was to be learned from watching his dad scorn stultifying, skulking, tasseled-tumbleweed in the fallow field of life.

Joseph Meehan advanced alright in his new class. His teacher Miss Ryan identified intelligence in Joseph. School became very challenging now, meeting older dinky girls and boys all bashful made Joseph very happy. Miss Ryan cotidalized allowance for Joseph's mammy – she magically guided Joseph's etymological mulling.

Dr. Patricia Sheehan tied Joseph hands onto her swimming togs and positioned him in the pool. Joseph moved lightly in the water holding Dr. Sheehan's shoulder strap, in water heated comfortably he dragged himself along and swam for the first time in his life. Swimming gave Joseph Meehan great pleasure. Dr. Sheehan seeing this got more tubes and put one on Joseph. Happily she sent him cruising up the pool where a Physiotherapist awaited him. Turning Joseph she sent him dreamily down the pool again. Halfway down he heeled over and his feet remained sticking-up out of the water. Dr. Sheehan pounced on him and adroitely hindered his sinking. Nothing daunted, he spent one of the most specially happy times of his life, thanks to a sympathetic, feeling lady.

Peace naturally breeds kindness, Joseph coted grass eating animals. He made nice happy plans. The lined chest, so deep, allowed maximum protection to the animals. Now none could say that Joseph Meehan had animals in snow mounds. He spent time, kindness and much love on his furry friends.

Joy hits a high level in lots of ways. Matthew Meehan found to say the kind thing almost always can isolate the tweed of irony. Joseph mattered nil to anyone looking-on. Matthew milled Joseph often in minding hidden, timid, joyous jostling in the hysterical hymn of life.

All people must question the quelling quest quietly, quoting Milton's Paradise Lost, attempting all quarrelling quests quisling quintain qualms queenly quiz. Joseph Meehan thought too of his poetry, he wondered about the logic of his art. His was a very hazardous undertaking as he had to fiercely fight a frightening handicap, a foolish facial expression and a doubtful public.

Nora Meehan noticed now Joseph's nightly, timid, lonely periods of illness, nose blocked, listless lethargic Joseph struggled in vain to breathe, lost in the trembling, terrible, lonely night. Slow incredulity cried keep me alive as Joseph accosted sincere Nora. Veganin tablet crushed on a spoon and melted with water he found helpful. Nora talked, told jokes or sometimes counted in an effort to distract Joseph. Only when relaxed could he unclench his teeth sufficiently to allow Nora to give him the medicine. Bathing in lukewarm water cooled his very hot and burning body. Another night had been turned from lonely tragedy, lost mercy, insecure penance, into another lovely lush oasis.

No route sign meant lots of hardship for poor Nora. She always left the house very early to gain advantage over the traffic. Matthew always put petrol in the car and tested it for oil and water before letting Nora and Joseph set out for Banagher. Yvonne had finished National School in Clontarf and had now happily domiciled in school. Sisters of La Sainte Union des Sacres

Coeurs, beautifully educated too, sculptured young, highly Madonna-handsome girls into young lissom ladies. Yvonne was allowed home one week-end in each month, so, happily Joseph and Nora drove to Banagher to collect her. Auntie Kathleen who also taught in the convent, lived near Banagher and comfort, cake and cooking were in wonderous happy happy evidence whenever Joseph called.

Joseph Meehan always took lovely interest in cooking. He missed not being able to kick football, climb trees, string chestnuts or speak on the telephone, but each silent lock it hastened into place opened Joseph's docile brain, live with busy-butted brilliant ideas.

Matthew Meehan looked tired, during the long irksome day he brought consolation and sympathy to many mild, pallid psychiatric patients. An open discussion was taking place in the C.R.C. School and Nora had been invited. Nora always gave Joseph his tea but had no time this evening. Matthew obliged by feeding sulky Joseph. Mothers have a knack which lovely dads can never hope to acquire.

All men mull over hell. Land lovers count their acres, monied folk count their millions but wise men count their cold, holy crosses. And that is the central core of our existence on this earth. Into cold, lonely hell came Joseph Meehan, all lost forever, spoiled at life's beginning and callously left beside calm timid Matthew and Nora Meehan.

Although Nora Meehan now knew about Joseph's interest in cooking, she was as yet unaware of his difficulty in putting together all letters appearing, particularly certain letters. Each day at reading children could read to all the class, but all Joseph could do was listen. Nora helped him at home, taking each word she explained how to leave out the unimportant letters and get the sound of the word from the remaining letters. Miss Ryan helped enormously by accruing lots more knowledge about the art of recognizing words. What neither Miss Ryan nor Nora knew was Joseph could only see because of his haphazard experience in reading, many words turned backwards . . . for example – Press – he would see a mirror impression looking like

– sserP – which always confused him. Joseph would then change the letters sserP, using his fingers to remember which letter went first – thumb became P, etc, and so he taught himself to recognize the word.

Joseph nolonger explained his ideas, irrevocably irately he milled instructions to Nora by utilizing his eyes. She endeavoured to understand, enthusiastically she apparently understood. Increasingly incredibly, incongruously she incorrigibly invited impertinent, irrelevant collation of identical ideologies. All oscillating lonely annihilating of lost dreams meant Joseph always anxiously aimed to allay his human failings and philosophically accepted his handicap.

Irritation with Charles Kenny gave Joseph endless trouble. Tactless, sly Charles milled Joseph Meehan with insinuating, loutish, ratty, loud ridicule. Lots of lives deal maddening, immediate, dogged, cowed etching, but Joseph nettled lastingly through being unable to defend himself either verbally or physically. Initially Larry Atkin helped, Arthur Coen then took-over and boldly defended Joseph. School became satisfying now, lessons were challenging, and simple, thoughtful, ever loyal Arthur and friends helped Joseph Meehan out of timely Charles Kenny's webb. Nora Meehan helped too by consoling Joseph. Slowly she counted the number of times Charles Kenny accosted him and gradually she helped Joseph to control his temper and understand poor Charles' difficulties.

Athlone always took precedence over Dublin in Nora Meehan's eyes. All her family attended school at Our Lady's Bower. In later years she brought Yvonne and Joseph to see her old school and visit Cornamagh Cemetery, smiling lovingly as happy memories came crowding back of her parents John and Catherine Power.

Matthew Meehan amounted little help along the way for Nora as he had to wake early to go to work in St. Brendan's Hospital. Each day arrived, washing calm Joseph with new hope in man's fight to overcome his heinous handicap. All events in life leave a mark on society – life took time off where Joseph Meehan was concerned. Matthew excused himself in honest love, phoning Nora to check if everything was alright. Looking after Joseph was a thankless lifetime job for Nora.

All anonymous opportunities owe their life to God. Joseph endured lots of difficulties but thousands of opportunities looked over his happy horizon. Lonely eveningtide always brought longing – a longing to write his omens of ominous obedience obelisk.

School became a truly wonderful experience, learning History, Geography, English, Mathematics, Nature Study, Irish, Music and Religious Knowledge always looked after Joseph's mind and gave him plenty to think about.

Joseph Meehan allowed every electric impulse to rack his body. Matthew elected to live in Dublin near The Central Remedial Clinic in order that Joseph would be near his school. As each day passed electric impulses got stronger, maddening Joseph with time consuming spasms. In allowing each trembling limb to act lamely, leeringly; lettered lonely lackadaisical Joseph acquired a tranquil exterior.

School benignly brought better flowering fruits into Joseph's life. He attended C.R.C. all the time, firstly schooling was helped along then physiotherapy helped his limbs to develop normally. Dr. Patricia Sheehan who originally extracted his first feeble word – mmm aaa MAMA, endeavoured continuously to extract fresh sounds from Joseph's benign larynx.

Lost opportunities irked Joseph tremendously. One by one each evening ended with nothing of significance achieved. Attention to television programmes gained knowledge for Joseph in interesting, informative, infatuating lessons.

School enabled Joseph Meehan to experiment, exchanging fresh ideas with brilliant thoughtful teachers. Each evening emanated etches in elevated angelic appraisal of his acute trials. School lost lots of lovely educated pupils each year, they went to Intermediate School to continue their studies.

Often in changing, insecure times, offers of ominous omnipotence electrifies earnest, endless education and endeavour. All notable engaging thoughts endure endless, eternal, embarrassing assimilation. Happiness helps endearing, exciting, evidently lost causes to be changed into enlightening, elating, elevating experiences.

School enabled Joseph Meehan each day to learn lots especially about boys and girls endeavouring energetically, excitingly innovatingly, all knowingly to conquer their horrid handicaps. Enigmatically, egocentrically, acutely Joseph noticed alot of old people otherwise languidly opting-out of life, came to life and would renew their desire to live after meeting one helplessly horrendously handicapped in such a jostling and lovely boyhood.

Out of other lovely lives order came to lift the cross from Joseph Meehan's lame life. Out of one, onerous, once helpless, trying tribulation, emerged all angrily an enigma. Among his family and friends he caused consternation. Among life's fanfare of trials all trying he learned lessons in typing. Among lovely events in his naturally-normal life Joseph made the acquaintance of a young bearded national teacher. Mr. O'Mahony always omitted to think of himself and attended to his pupils needs. At awkward moments in Joseph's life he lovingly stepped-in, answering for him and asking the questions which Joseph would love to ask himself. He brought all Joseph's class on an outing on board a fishing trawler. Each pupil met all the crew and were allowed to inspect the sacred hamradio room. All allowances were made for Joseph and he was manually carried on a conducted tour of the boat.

Amending idle, tame, troublesome, Lona Nolan's ankle gave Dr. Barry lots of annoyance. He loved lonely handicapped children, answering alone across a dreadful distance – meaning a life's ambition to happily help all frantic paralysed patients.

Each day opened ordinary eyes in schooling, educating and training bodies in locating all energy in pursuit of physical climes. Every avenue was explored in an attempt to arrive at God's feet and abounding mercy. Every day allowed Joseph Meehan ease in school – every accommodation was allowed in simple hope that a means of communication might possibly be found for sad, silent Joseph.

Another year brought another teacher, Miss Hannaway. She

lovingly helped everybody to learn all about Confirmation. She explained the significance of the sacrament and of God's gift of The Holy Spirit. The morning of Confirmation dawned bright and sunny. Lemon-gold light streamed into the cathedral-like church through its vast arched windows. Joseph, his hair lit by bright sunlight sat along with his father who was to act as his son's sponsor during the ceremony. Music milled from the organ as the bishop arrived. Mass commenced, amidst languid music confirmation was conferred. Allowing gainful knowledge to overcome him, Joseph Meehan elected to eerily elicit exclusive excuses, looking outside himself for identity in life's lovely landscaped land.

One day took precedence over all others in Joseph's life. Always anticipating, allocating allowances and allotments, anointing angry aching acute intuition, he moaned and prayed into the early hours of morning. That day Miss Keating lovingly informed Nora Meehan of a new anti-spastic drug Lioresal, which had come on the market just a week previously. Miss Keating was doing physiotherapy on lonely Joseph's painriddled hip. Nora agreed to consult Dr. Barry about the drug and about Joseph's lazy hip.

Among life's indigent agnostics Joseph Meehan finally found refuge and isolation. He coaxed God, he angelically prayed, always comforting himself with the hope of finally abriging apparent aseptic areas of aggravating attitudes. Attics erected conveniently in haggards of words eat into holes in his mind.

Accounts arriving at the datacentre in The C.R.C. announced every Christmas – "Party for children in 'All Purposes Room' at close of school". All mention of Christmas over-whelmed children with wild axioms of once lonely lost eventide now away in the past. Against always glittering multicoloured tinsel and gleaming Christmas tree lights, agile folk invited wheelchair-bound friends to dance and everybody swayed to glorious, magical music. On unedited office C.R.C. appeals Lady Valerie Goulding lovingly allowed elected agents to allocate all other parties for friends of hers, but she attended in person the Children's Party, where she catered, danced and gleefully let her hair down.

Mankind always amuses himself by foolish conjecture, on odious old ones, oceans mated on opal-shattered, oil-saturated satellites and from which all oligarchies once alighted. Joseph thought too, only lordly thinking, turned thoughts towards tiresome trends, in tinges of tranquil trying tremors of titular timidity, sorrow turned to triumph.

Only Joseph Meehan knew kicking football was out, his dastardly daring, misshapen, though accurate foot wreaked havoc on the football pitch. Only when someone propelled his wheelchair for him, pushing and allowing Joseph to kick the ball – making it feasible for him to play football. Only endless patience could help Joseph and in this world of squandering and oxen-minded indifference towards others less talented he unbelievably found marvellous, helpful Nora.

Matthew Meehan all courageously accompanied Joseph on countless and tiring outings. If there was a mountain to be climbed Matthew lifted his handicapped son onto his broad shoulders and joyfully set-out for the mountain top. Among his family, lovely idyllic idle feasting often obliterated obvious manual annihilation of monotony.

Joseph Meehan milled pills called Phenobarbitone into his system, attempting to pull idle if incisive electrical spasms into old-fashioned working order. Only offering little explanation of Lioresal side-effects, Dr. Barry introduced Joseph very gradually to the new drug. Initially the dosage was small but Joseph could feel an alteration akin to miracle-making, all his dreams were about to dam-burst.

All lonely moonlight nights found Joseph only lonelier still. Poor notable Nora listed any apparent changes in Joseph's behaviour. All changes included illuminating insights into tired tricky tooling, saving alot of ominous IBM typing from Joseph Meehan's schooling having nothing accresced. Alighting from the lonely lost loose lancerated lettered level of thinking, earthing electrical elevated elated alleviating words, Joseph's ballad of life's wilful woolly wade across illness all offensive, solumnly seemed staple Solstice.

Out of terrible ordeals life nonetheless marks out assorted

offings, anodyne always cymballed Joseph Meehan's angel guar-
dian. Every lonesome look lessened Jesus Christ's Crucifixion in
Joseph's eyes. He had happily accepted crucifying handicap but
begged for some form of communication with which to express
his alert, myriad, brilliant, milling mind. Balls of fiery frantic
despair struck Joseph's every attempt to type. First his left hand
failed, then his right, attempts with both feet achieved nothing.
Eva Fitzpatrick his typing teacher then thought of his mouth and
instructed him in the use of a suck and blow method on a Possum
Machine – it was all to no avail. In the meantime Roisin had
given an electric typewriter to Nora Meehan, instructing her in
its use and lovingly encouraging Joseph to practise at home.
Minus was Joseph's achievement on immediately tackling type-
writing on home territory. Nora accepted defeat and put away
the typewriter. Eva and Catherine designed a chin-stick, assum-
ing that Joseph might manage to type with his chin. Another
disappointment dimmed their hopes. At each staff meeting fail-
ure was reported to Dr. Barry, but he lovingly would not accept
defeat where Joseph was concerned. On each occasion he told
his wonderful staff "we must keep trying". As a last hope, a
Unicorn-like head piece was designed for Joseph, in vain hope
that he might somehow manage to type with his head. Moves to
practise placing the typing stick on the correct letter always met
with constant, callous, milling defeating spasms. Wonderful
hopes sadly dashed as spasm upon spasm moulded Joseph's last
attempt to turn sad sweet sanity stable. Poor Eva never knew
what Joseph was going through as she undauntedly assisted him
with dastardly dallient posers as to how to best his spasms. New
lasting despair gripped Joseph and hastened his desire to commit
suicide, but even that form of escape was denied him. A paper-
thin balance between total rejection of God and acceptance of
God's Will somehow still existed in Joseph's mind. It was on a
vesper too long to describe that Joseph Meehan finally dozed
off to sleep. He had gone to bed at his usual hour but stayed
awake praying and begging God to have pity on him. Morning
was breaking before sleep came – listlessly lying limp he felt the
touch of a kiss on his cheek. He swiftly opened his eyes and

glanced all about the room – nobody was there! Mystified, Joseph slipped into sleep again. All Joseph's longings lost lustre as glorious sleep took over his consciousness. Life always anchors lost lonely ambitions and soon it more than mastered dead dreams for Joseph. Mindful of his frantic despair, Joseph dreamed that he was dead. Mankind's corpse immortalizes God's image left with the world's dark doubters and in his acute dreams, Joseph dreamt that night that he saw God and His Blessed Mother. They were dressed as modern man giving a handsomeness to their hair style. All was sweetness, serenity, answering Joseph's enquiring gaze. Casting honest aching eyes downwards Joseph saw a grey typewriter sitting on the floor. He instinctively looked back at God and solely Lady Mary.

Nora Meehan was assuaging Matthew's acute lack of a son's looming valiant vessel of ovary selection creation, but baring mankind, malice laughed mollifying preening.

Weetabix used at breakfast time Joseph Meehan found provided quick energy and certified fast lovely reliable rousing. All foods appealed to Joseph but steak cooked very rare was his favourite. Cheese sandwiches, toasted golden-brown often provided quick nourishing snacks, assuring sincere Nora of calm mind about Joseph's intake of vitamins.

Nora now noticed a marked improvement in gesticulating Joseph. She reported back to Dr. Barry and he gradually built-up the dosage. Mesmerized by the changes which he alertly detected in himself, Joseph found currents as strong as electric power, now nolonger able to squander all his strength. Spasms still moidered him, but now he was free of those dreadful deadly currents which un-nerved him as they butchered their callous route from his cranium via his spine to hotly roust his left foot dashing away as wickedly as they had come.

Every day came, more slowly and more gradually things began to happen, mollifying lonely lost longings, fastening fresh lovely dashing onto sad dreams. Joseph cast high dashing along lonesome fiords of irate illusions, dashing loose solitude with lousy, onerous omens of high, deadly-molten dams.

Mankind endows nothing that God has not terrifyingly nurtured all through millenniums of years. Lonely, lovely, dear Douglas Cambell's fast death during the long-holiday week-end frightened Joseph. Mourning lonely life's limp lovely Douglas – sadly, Joseph lovingly carried on his iota of lonesome hallucination. Young, naturally-normal Douglas's life daily meant annihilation, sardonically achieving endurable and abundance of mead. Offering acute odes – Joseph endowed obdurate, blighted Douglas's death.

Tobacco-smells lost all accrued scent as Uncle Patsy Meehan smilingly finished his cigar prior to his leaving for his flight to Leeds. Corpus Christi parish attested admirably to the fulsome usage of diligent Fr. Meehan's polished endeavours over the years. Joseph and Yvonne were always sorry to see their eloquacious uncle pose as not feeling lonely, as he casually said goodbye, for another year's holiday had dashed delightfully away.

Along lonesome hazardous avenues of attics, axed out terrifyingly from gardens growing wild with amazing flowery words, travelled Joseph Meehan, mingling muses, aspirations, castles, lords – Paradise moved as carismatically motivated medicine.

Matthew Meehan mollified all lost pining pity associated all harrowingly, raspingly with looking on saviour-like at salient manhood mated amicably, stoically to life in a Mental Hospital. Alternate days saw Matthew lord among his friendly animals, as though life salved his sadness he returned to his friendly fireside leopard calm. Lonely sadness lost – peace always came fast as Matthew worked on his farm.

Evoking solace from youth frowning left no mark on God's lovely doorway to Heaven. Joseph Meehan sampled dilatable delights every time he drollingly played God friendly, fulsome fears of frolicsome flashes of foibles. Malleable, long, laborious, monumental manoeuvring looked like bearing daring round panegyrics, among passing deadly free iodoform from full, pulsating, slowly diabolically-ploughed land ... travelled Joseph Meehan.

Eva Fitzpatrick lovingly pondered on Lioresal's possibilities towards tying-back poor frantic Joseph Meehan's jeering, jerky spasms. On a visit to Dr. Barry, lasting loves led Joseph to call on his old friends Kathleen Keating his special sweet physiotherapist and Eva Fitzpatrick his sweet special typing teacher. Other lonely days pulled poor Eva to point-out the necessity of typing peacefully, dramatically, as slim slow hope of caging frivolous spasms now sportingly seemed possible. Nora moved the typewriter into position on her folding-leaf kitchen table. The height of the table was right but the light table was inclined to heel over. Nora undaunted by the problem balanced the table by placing all her upturned kitchen stools, her clothes iron and Matthew's shot-putt practice weight on the opposite end to the heavy typewriter. Past poor efforts played lonely plodding losses before Joseph's moist, timid-looking, looming, nasty estoppel. Nora pontificated, poor Joseph laughed to himself, galling poor Nora even more. On his next visit to Eva he had to admit about his slovenly, gelatinous, brazen strike. Another reminder from Eva moved Joseph to mingle hopely longings with zealous, piercing platitudes.

Matthew and Yvonne had gone to town, illustrating the typing machine Nora instigated proceedings, instructing astounded Joseph to carry-on, she cushioned his sad chin in her cosy cupped hands. Putting hidden fears behind him he solemnly aimed his head-stick at the letters pouring into his mind. He hopefully had planned poetically wording old slights and insulting, belittling experiences accrued easily in his life. Nora rigged-up the paper and surreptitiously watched as Joseph typed...

I Learn To Bow

> Polarized I was paralysed,
> Plausibility palated,
> People realized totally,
> Woefully once I totally
> Opened their eyes.

Nora passed her hand all shakingly over Joseph's hair and looking sweetly through years' accrued tears she enquired

"Joseph is that the sort of a mind you have?" Joseph manfully looked understandingly, lovingly, joyfully from Nora towards the ceiling giving his affirmative signal over and over and over again. Joseph now felt power nudging playfully, incredibly, honourably, lovingly, eruptingly, solemnly, relievingly in his honest heart. Moping was not to attain anything, so Joseph launched into literary fields, pillaging places, putting irreplaceably out of line, creations forming word's meaning. Nora brought light into added focus. Groping Medusa-like, satirically Joseph moulded alot of normal, naughty knowledge into typewritten pages. Nora moved the typewriter in and out from the lounge to the kitchen table more or less at Joseph's command. Oftentimes the trip was for nothing, only bulls-eye fastness of all beautiful direction, could manoeuvre to capture pouring, pounding, pulverizing ideas.

Nora made arrangements with Miss Ryan the newly appointed principal to allow Joseph to remain in the C.R.C. School for another year. He was only eleven years old and dear Miss Ryan kindly allowed him to repeat sixth class again. Petite Angela Keane was his mod-dressed new teacher. Kindness gimleted her emanating laughing, ponderous pottage of copious clouds of camel-loitering, lovely moding. Bold Miss Keane and Joseph candidly passed delightful foibles indirectly from one to the other without any of the other members of the class being aware of it. Money-lessons always made accounts-gossip in class. Joseph called collectively members of his class looking on, old school chums, delightfully lovely, who faithfully plagued Miss Keane for pious, poor, catastrophic life's vivid, monotonous, looming youthful fruits. Miss Keane lovingly gave-in, all lessons manhandled, into elysium loitered her clumsy class.

Joseph continued to write all happily, jeering all, poking fun at hazards life buoyantly hoisted, ahoying manfully lively doom's lovely fanfare of feebleness.

Mr. John Kelly, always sure of interest obviously found Joseph's language surprising. He nurtured the early attempts in writing and showed Joseph how to outline his stories. English class always seemed to come alive whenever tall, mighty John Kelly's head appeared round the classroom door.

Joseph Meehan looked at the long letter patiently waiting for Nora to prise it open and reveal Uncle Patsy's all lovely news. Letting something fall, Nora stooped down to retrieve a cutting from a newspaper and looking at Joseph she read "Literary Contest For The Handicapped" – his enquiring alert gaze allowed Nora to read on and all smilingly give the information he so obviously sought. Interest in schooling his carefree, careless concatenate mind looked lordly across his salient manhood, lessening hotly-aroused acetous longings. Lively close attention to the closing date exacerbated Joseph's battling brain.

Matthew Meehan and Yvonne lessened Joseph's purgatory, all loves led ahead a listless emaciated fellow-man whom society discarded. Yvonne allowed for Joseph's disability and mixed laughter, foolery, fighting and love, polishing dankerous, dead, sad sorrows dredging, with oldfashioned machinery called "zealous caring for others".

America goaded Aunt Eva and Uncle Joe Power to lovely action. Nora always kept in touch with her father's brother and his Scottish-born wife. Each Christmas arrived bringing with it an airmail envelope, very neatly addressed to Joseph and containing lovely sweet Christmas wishes and salutary news of a Novena of Masses being offered, spiralling to a magnificent all solemn High Mass at The Grotto of The Nativity in Bethlehem on Christmas Day. Joseph always found thanks lost meaning when he was unable to rightly express it himself – all lovingly he now asserted himself and typed dear Grandaunt Eva a sincere personal letter of special warm thanks. Hardly had disastrous news brought listless Joseph lopping sad, sorrowful branches from his family tree when he all fastidiously had to feel sweet relief at hearing that his dear Grandaunt had passed peacefully in her slumbers.

"Title of Article or Poem" read The Spastics Society Literary Contest form – Joseph serenely filled-in all the details. Last minute checking and all poor dreams assisted his entry as it winged its way to London. Nora answered weakly as the special, delightful, happy phonecall brought the news "Joseph has won a special prize, his entry being judged as a work beyond comparison". Much questions were asked as Nora revealed the lively news, one particular query cropped up again and again "where does Joseph get his vocabulary?". Nora could certainly not give a very satisfactory reply. Dalliently, joyfully, Joseph longed to be able to say that he only knew that as he typed thoughts, brilliant, bright, boiling words poured into his mind, sometimes with such ferocity that he felt spoiling confusion creep across his turbulent, creative mind.

Flight EI.172 swiftly taxied down the run-way before eventually taking off on its flight to London. Joseph and Nora made themselves comfortable and dearly desired a safe flight. Aer Lingus hostesses served tea or coffee, Joseph thankfully refused any refreshments and slowly took-in every detail associated with flying. All heaven slowly owed mingling clouds full offerings, powering alone mighty skies' skills at maple-leaf designed sad scrolls, ornamenting bold snow-white, cotton-wool landscapes outside Joseph's little window. Arriving at Heathrow Airport – lovely captain Moran invited Joseph to look into that rarely viewed cock-pit and showed him an array of instruments, clocks, dials and lights which fairly took his breath away.

Lunch at 12.30 on Wednesday June 28th at the International Students House in Great Portland Street, London and the reception afterwards for prizes to be given will be at The Spastics Society's headquarters – the judges, Lady Wilson, Mrs. Edna Healey, Lord Willis and Michael Randolph who is editor of the *Reader's Digest* will be there to meet the winners – Joseph could feel his heart thumping as he pondered purposefully on the letter which he received telling him of his schedule for possibly, unbelievably the greatest day in his life.

Mrs. Edna Healey looked beautiful as she arrived for the prizegiving ceremony. Joseph Meehan purposefully looked at her, as she it was who judged his entry of prose and poetry and had so happily recommended his being awarded a special prize. Cameras flashed, reporters took hasty fortuitous statements from all poor amused Nora. Joseph's all tremendous, wonderful,

awe-inspiring moment came when Mrs. Healey stepped towards
him to present him with his beautiful Ingersoll Quartz Wrist
Watch. A tall dark haired man stepped forward, he was intro-
duced to Joseph as Mr. Bill Wright, producer of one of Joseph's
favourite quiz shows, Mastermind, and on behalf of his team
presented their avid viewer with a specially lovely gift. There
was still another paralysing surprise bewilderingly in store for
Joseph Meehan. Mrs. Edna Healey delightfully invited him to
visit her at her home – No. 11, Downing Street, the official
residence of The Chancellor of The Exchequer. Nora and Joseph
hurriedly changed prior to being taken on a tour of lovely
London by The Spastics Society and which was to end at Down-
ing Street. Mrs. Healey, dressed in a frock of fresh green, opened
the door of No. 11 and extended a lovely quiet welcome to
Joseph Meehan. Taking him on a personally conducted tour she
filled-in all the wonderful accounts associated with the history
and previous personages who through the centuries had lived or
visited in her architecturally beautiful home. A visit to the home
of The Prime Minister of Great Britain at No. 10 Downing
Street was hurriedly and secretly arranged by lovely, thoughtful
Mrs. Healey. Joseph and Nora pleasantly found themselves on
a whirl-wind tour of No. 10. Sincerely, Joseph tried to thank
Mrs. Healey for the golden, glorious hour which he had spent
with her.

The End

5 September 1978 – 8 February 1979

158, Vernon Ave.,
Clontarf, D.3.
21st August 1977

Dear Aunt Eva,

I bet you never thought you would be hearing from me! Aunt Eva and Uncle Joe, roughly three weeks ago I was put on a new drug called Lioresal, it is an anti-spastic drug. I find it wonderful.

To think that I would be able to write to you was beyond my wildest dreams. The drug relaxes my muscles even when I am typing.

You were great to think of me all over the years since I was born. Having Mass said for me at Bethlehem rewarded me through the hard times I remember. I wish to thank you both.

How is Joseph and Marion and the children? I am eleven years of age now and am in sixth class in school. You have heard about Yvonne in Banagher, she is doing very well. She is doing her Intermediate Examination next June. I miss her when she is away as I have no one to fight with, ha, ha.

Hope you and Uncle Joe are keeping well.

That is all for now.

Love
Christy.

158, Vernon Avenue,
Clontarf, D.3.
22nd/8/'77

Dear Uncle Patsy,

I feel sure you will be surprised to hear from me. I prayed for so long for this day that it seemed it would never come. Rain usually comes before sunshine, Lioresal came before my break-through. Pity the tablets were not out long ago. First thing I want to do is to thank you for praying for me all down the years.

A tip of my stick to the keys opens a whole new world-oasis for me.

Kathleen spent a few days with us in Dublin, she was getting her teeth out.

A set of silent movies are being shown on T.V. they are very funny. Soon you will be home again, but I will be back at the C.R.C. I am pleased to be making headway at last.

That is all for now.

Yours sincerely,
Christy.

158, Vernon Avenue,
Clontarf, Dublin. 3.
3rd July 1978

Mrs. Heycock,
The Spastics Society,
London.

Dear Mrs. Heycock,

Occasionally I meet many a kind person, but on my recent royal trip to London I experienced calm dignity, which almost moved me to tears.

I wear my watch very manfully, each awkward gleefull glance conjures up magical memories of London and The Spastics Society, its members and its kindness to my mother and myself.

Please accept my sincere gratitude and also that of my mother. We were most impressed by your thoughtfulness. Please convey our loving wishes and deep gratitude to all in Fitzroy Square.

Yours sincerely,
Christy Nolan

I Learn To Bow

Polarized, I was paralysed,
Plausibility palated,
People realized totally,
Woefully, once I totally
Opened their eyes.

20 August 1977

I Peer Through Ugliness

Years dead tears, peter down my face,
Lucifer quietly plays me down,
Out of a light there came Christ Divine,
Peace always comes, reigns awhile.
Day after dawn, raw quiet rested there,
As I peered through rough pastures,
Dew drops glistened in golden buttercups.

I wrote the above poem because every day I realized more and more how handicapped I was.

22 August 1977

Mothers

Parents are people whose lives are physically and mentally linked to their children. Women rear large families and fathers earn the money necessary to support them.

A mother however plays a very important role, she it is who teaches her child the first lesson on life. My mother is especially lovely, as it was she who encouraged me down the years. A fiery person would be no use to me, only patience could help a spastic. People will never know what she really did, she consoled me when I was sad, she played with me when I was glad, she taught me all I know about people and their problems. A person finds other friends in life, but nobody will ever replace their mother.

31 August 1977

Dad

Who is dad, or what is he?,
Only I can tell,
He is the man that reaches –
God love him may I say,
For life and hope and so
Happy looks he too,
You'd never think
He was only just my dad.

4 September 1977

On Remembering The Beara Landscape

Lakes and rivers, lovely scenery,
Parks and skies, mountain greenery,
A lovely day awaiting.
Away we drive through lonely roads,
Late Fall played a tune on our motor car,
We laughed and sang as we sped along,
Pores open wide along polar jaws.
A possie occurred riding,
Along lonely laneways speeding,
A herd of cattle steaming,
Which brought us to a halt.
A paper passed on an ethereal, rapier-like wind,
A song bird flew on fiery wing,
Over hill and dale clouds billowed,
Dancing the dance of golden dreams.

I spent a lovely holiday with my family on The Beara Peninsula in West Cork and upon returning home I wrote the above poem.

14 September 1977

My Ambitions

Taste of pity as people stare,
Love, lots of love from mother,
Pills you find as lasting prayer,
An irate person may possibly
Have faith, instead of despair.

18 September 1977

Boring People

The point about people being boring is that they put no interest in finding out what other people think. Regardless of person's feelings they blow on and on, pointing their son's progress as purpose for vain glory. There are other people too, who love the sound of their own voices and rise my temper by ranting and raving. Then, there is the friendly one who loves petting you like a hairy dog.

2 October 1977

A Pass To Your Dead

A grave that always waits,
A verge round at front and
A lasting sad cross,
Put away sadness,
Pray all the while,
Past is sorrow,
Heaven will be thine.

My uncle Fr. Patsy asked me to write a poem for him – I wrote the above.

13 October 1977

Hey Patrick, Olé

As those friends of mine grew up they virulently boohed puppy-love and tut tutted when I asked "can I join rugged lovely Roary in go-karting".

People asked me for a reason for living as dogs leaped across

my paralysed limbs and sadly I said "do not ask for food from
a starving man".

Years were tearing asunder my aspirations of becoming top
man youth leader in Saturday's treasure appearance, but sibling
hopes ring a weary dirge. Patrick looked number one now, for
great go-karter that he was, he zealously zig zagged speedily
down the narrow zany slopes. Around towering associations
friends combine all their pious wishes in procuring a prize of a
lovely laser-sharp lance. Most of my friends thought I was tardy
with my congratulations, but Patrick understood. A man needs
lovely lasting lessons to make a fast friend.

16 October 1977

Milk

A pint a day far outweighs a pint of the other! I put milk in my
tea, milk in my coffee, milk in my cocoa, milk in my cereal and
milk for a drink. Can you find that many uses for the other?

As rats sagely watch grain grow the cows graze greedily on
lush green grass lowing loudly as milking time draws near. A
signal from the farmer alerts the boss cow and she sets out for
the farmyard with all the rest trailing after her.

Activity builds up as milking starts. Smells of fresh milk is all
about. Dairy work strains the milk, leaving lots of foaming filmy
froth. Lorries bring the milk in a daily collection to the creamery
where it is bottled. From there the milkman collects it and
delivers on our doorstep.

Pleasure erupts as a fresh bottle of celestial, creamy, calorie-
packed milk pours out, rising a rose-speckled dish of weetabix
to royal frizz.

> A pail of milk so astonishing,
> Onerous liquid, verily marvellous,

> Each date does a sage sail,
> Swiftly down a ravenous tongue.

My prize-winning entry in The National Dairy Council Schools
Competition. My first time ever to win a prize ... a camera!

23 October 1977

Mammy

Far out in space planets lie
Asleep, potash appearing
Along between iron layers
Embellished coral reefs deep below oceans,
All the pluto-alert antennae were
Electric with the news,
A mammy arrived on a place,
A round earth,
Pearl alone on the land below.

4 November 1977

Death

Pallid, cold, heart operating
Once, was sadly sore to-day,
Alone, tears slide down my old man's face,
I am roaming o'er my life,
A part lamenting cannot change,
A Paradise Moses worked for
Seeks a deep equilibrium,

A real art, a peace always apparent.
Love so old reforms friends,
Appearing to many as will allow,
Peace plays such a role,
A treasure only surely sapespered
During the dolorous days of death.

8 November 1977

Dad and Mam

Light and fair and lazy,
Permanent, tested, passing,
All established, all calamity,
All zealous, all landed,
All swearing, all dazzling,
All beastly deadly smothering,
All affected.
Pall, peasant sad dear sprees,
All not allowed to ferment,
All, because of dad and mam.

I am describing myself for others. My mam and dad understood my lonely,
lost life as no one else could.

18 November 1977

My Earliest Memories of The C.R.C.*

A loser all the way,
A leap in the C.R.C.,
A look past all a man
Appears to be.

*C.R.C.   Central Remedial Clinic.

All my blood ran cold at first, leaving me a brain-damaged, all paralysed pauper, appearing to foolish, ignorant people as "heaven's reject".

Wonderful, loving Hon. Lady Goulding and her C.R.C., assured, calmed and created a new me. Fresh fond associations tried to sympathise with my emerging denegation. A team of specialists took me in hand. Dr. Barry agreed with my parents, that my alert brain was the only thing ticking-over in my body. Dr. Sheehan and her bag of tricks, made her first appearance one day as I lay on the floor having physiotherapy. As she produced each object I crowed with great joy. She allowed me all the top delight of producing my first word mmm aaa MAMA.... Just imagine my delight.

Psychologists then carried out I.Q. tests, hastening all parent paediatric allowances to tackle a power pool, offering massive promise to young spastics.

> A school to own you,
> A special school,
> A paradise of real order,
> A tale to praise everyone.

23 November 1977

Christmas

> Pies of mincemeat,
> An ear asleep,
> A smell of cooking,
> A merry feast,
> A meaty turkey,
> A roasting aroma,
> Apron oligarchy.
> A post quota,

A priest at prayer
A tasselled altar.

8 December 1977

The Crib

A cold, cold tale,
To treasure.

Snow fell dreamily, healthily, mottledy, in alarming spasms, covering the precipitous route to Bethlehem. Joseph and Mary left Galilee, a peasant couple, a pass allocated assigning them to the Caesar Augustus part of Judea. There, their tale began. Mary's baby Jesus Christ was born, an earth's saviour, cradled among an ass and an ox. Shepherds learned the wonderful tidings from an angel of the God Father in heaven. They came to Bethlehem and adored the Almighty Redeemer of the world.

People remember Bethlehem,
As tender, tangible amelioration.

4 January 1978

Mote In Other Hands

An era garrulous,
A rape scare,
An effluence real,
Man.
Drink, all rapid
Arsenic to youth.

13 January 1978

A Man

Red Sea land and
Red Sea rapine,
Red Sea all anxious,
Red Sea aches,
Red Sea spoils,
Red Sea pirates.
Red Sea appearing
Red, replenished,
Red Sea lonely,
Red Sea treachery.

19 January 1978

War

Apple Pie,
Women to aorist,
Alone betwixt love
And dreadful carnage,
All moat alimony,
Manpower sonant,
All motes roaming,
All blood flowing,
Down the river of life.

23 January 1978

Old Age

A person looking down a life-time sees a passing army reel along. In the army, each soldier represents an event in a person's life. Geriatric awareness awakens beautiful and vivid memories of each event.

Man always wonders about the autumn of his life, he erroneously yearns for time's opera to stand still. A man questions the wonders Pompeii locked away, but tide and time revealed its message. As it was with Pompeii so it is with old age, each old person stores wonderful accounts and wonderful stories of an era long gone.

Mars' appearance questions all rational use of lasting euthanasia. Surely, if we can scan Mars by our knowledge and use of Science, we should be able eventually to work towards easing the final years man has left before darkness.

28 January 1978

Trees Roan

Naught ought be suggested,
Eulogized, penurized,
Honoured and nurtured,
More orange appearing,
Emblazoned, meandering,
Mad red, land brown,
Meadow green,
Mellow yellow,
Are the colours
Of the roan trees.

8 February 1978

Snowflakes

Snow – lovely snow,
For lord and lady,
Now and piano,
Nolonger malady,
Party maffia,
Amicable map,
Melody on marquetry
Photography all marly,
Arson man opens,
Opera, play solo,
A god in mephitis,
No melancholy.

9 February 1978

More About Clan Nolan

My mother and my father lean,
My ever fastidious sister,
Make love creep all sweet;
Mewll-like, a beautiful basic
Molecule, appearing on the
Pampered planet of earth,
Pulmonary Lobsided,
Mammy and Sister and Daddy:
Among them, ambulatory I become
Much bolstering did relieve:
Tears of joy flowed down faces,
Miracle of miracles, endurance
Paid, all heaven opened and
Down it came – a pill so small –
Desert cultivated. Molar locked

Molar head-on, poetry mute
Under solemn poem, wander where
You go, word langets. No map
Could mood the sure poise,
All moves among, and sounds
More gay, comb more hair –
Measure it, jagged pair may
Loan a pot. Men may compose
Poetry prose or literature,
Veritable angels' wings now
Number nought, under morning
Moons, all nomads pray
Nothing mean, nothing naughty
Moves mortuary. Beauty lost
Loves no person, nothing daunts
Madness, nothing loves baseness,
Monstrous man makes murderous
Machines, readily non-necessary:
More about Christy Nolan's
Patter, poor artist that is
In me, my manner looks dumb;
Mother found the key –
Understanding nods opened eyes
Lacking enormous tame imaginings;
No matter where I wander, no
Reason and monetary motion
Could make all meaning, no
Natural order could excuse, no
Man equate, what Mother brought
Out – no one may relish.
Motes know their Open Sesame
Altar, more ought to ponder
And muse on this most of all –
Monolithic monument may move
Mountains, more in earnest.

18 April 1978

May

All spoilt beauty
All comes to darn,
All songs sung
All nature moans,
All nubile approaches
All gad plans,
All nocturnal animals
All move silently.
All lordly moorland
All manners nourish,
All cold accounts
All tread past.
All nature melts
All months' comas,
All lumber makes
All pomegranate manna
All meseems convenient.
All meantime
All mace pan
All transparent,
All manner amicable
All mercy Monday
All moans bold
All roved manoeuvring,
All Noah noted
All May abuts.

2 May 1978

Pope Paul VI

Man's coldest dream –
And amidst all –
And antithesis –
And absolution.

And mankind
And mortuary –
And burial –
And lonesome.

Pope Paul VI died to-day – above poem contains a few of my thoughts.

6 August 1978

Donegal

Quiet, quiet-
Queer quest,
Another quandary.

Another, amicable-
Queenly,
Another, almost-
Animal.

Another aiming –
Another, a quiet-
Anchorage,
Another, queencalm.

Another lovely-
Quest, opulent,

Aquafresh blue,
Another amethyst.

The above poem describes the sights, sounds and puzzling encounters of a caravan holiday in Donegal.

10 August 1978

Marjorie Wallace

Amen –
And obsequies –
A year's dream –
Accrued –
A baby.

M.s Wallace asked me to write a poem especially for her – she was pregnant at the time.

19 August 1978

My Dublin Bay

Mall beautiful,
Moon's pearly cut,
Municipal money
Municipal embay,
Many moorings
Moaning,
Maps not mawkish,
Many walk moodily
Dreaming.
Electric lights
Appease,

Among red all gas
Amber all low,
Amidst my dad, mam and sister,
I follow the tide's flow.

3 September 1978

Perangamo

A Short Story

Mankind meditates on lovely tear-making manners in other people.... Merimba rode towards Mesazem and Merimba rode in a mad red-bed Mercedes motorcar. Map markings placed Mesazem on a Roman boreen amid Roman toll guards. An everlasting murky grey beastly cloud followed the fast moving car as it sped all dangerously to Mesazem. Merimba looked at the rich coloured, foliaged, green verdure thoughtfully, looked at mad game scatter in ferocious mad panic and catapulted maniacally ahead.

Merimba Perangamo, a lustful lout to all who saw manliness as a desirable trait in a young man, meant more to his gorgeous wife than money or manliness could manage to provide. Merimba always meant more to Ruth, all paralysed, as she calmly sat passé, accompanied by a red-faced, ribald, wine swallowing, foul-mouthed woman. Ruth Eshuba to her parents rose all their hopes to rosy heights. All Ruth asked from her parents dearly came to her. She in a way found her parents' love stuffy, and longed for freedom. That day came when fate attracts a soul towards its destiny, she learned to her cost.

Morning broke forth in golden marble-decked skies, a beautiful peaceful cemetery, a dear soul alone stood heedlessly staring at a freshly-made brutal, brown grave. Merimba Perangamo, seeing far away from him a lone hunched figure, found fresh fear creeping through his fuzzy, very dead, dark lonely dawn. Merimba looked away, bastard that he seemed to be, he still could not approach a mad, frightened, but seemingly dead girl. Praying, something he frowned on greatly, joining grovelling honest hands and with zealous dilatory tears going pouring loosely, sadly down his face, he approached, dreading fiercely his coming gory revelation. He made faltering footsteps, loose limbs lagging lazily, non co-operatively behind.

Merimba Perangamo placed some flowers in an open, shaky,

very cold hand, and looking sorrowfully into lamb-sad amber eyes he said, "Naught can dare aspire to make earnest my honest obligation to help you Ruth". "Generations may all be buried in burial grounds" announced Ruth poignantly, "but my map points to this sole grave". Merimba lay great emphasis on his next words. "Ruth" he said "my aim, realize, is sadly solemnly to declare candidly my part in placing you in such a tragic position. A dark night it eventually turned out to be, giving fast driving dreadful foolhardy challenges. I made a decision to try scaring your father and mother with my daredevil driving. Recognizing their red car with its familiar number plate driving carefully towards home I frenetically found myself going more foolishly fast than usual. Narrowing the gap between us, I drove hussar-like round in front of them meaning to reve fiercely, swiftly getting out of their path. All God's goodness could not help face my car straight rapidly, the suddenness of the fierce fright caused your father to swerve too sharply, striking the ragged fence and careering panic stricken to a ferocious death on the rocks and water in the gorge below. Pulling my car to a very deliberate halt I numbly geared badly shaking legs to bring me down to the felonious death gorge. Unfortunately fire engulfed their car leaping deamon-like into the night."

Looking ghastly, ambling blindly, Merimba staggered away from the scene looking carefully for any giveaway surface marks on part of his car. Moaning amounting to malapert permanent tombs reverbations, flowed from passion and great gloom in his heart. Merimba Perangamo knew an awful mad moment of sheer rivetting panic, good parents' breeding and mercy forgotten, his main aim was to make a quick getaway.

A mottled, milky mean man reached Mullaserra, all weak, disturbed, sweating pools of mental poison. Merimba Perangamo all mad went towards the bar in his beautiful mansion, poured himself a large whiskey and mental oblivion looked nigh.

No peace could erase Merimba's mounting leopard-spotted damnation, he all anxiously appeared to Ruth at the cemetery and gabbled greedily, into lonely moribund all lost eyes. All Merimba moaned about, Ruth amounted a passing summary dumb silence, she feared feelings of doom and moaning all mournfully she groped her way from the cemetery.

Merimba Perangamo made his lonely way home fighting madly maddening undercurrents of electric thrombosis in his brain.

Merimba gave lots of thought to his next excuse for seeking Ruth Eshuba. Poor Ruth cried fulsome dolorous tears, each passing night brought fond poor memories flowing longingly. All saw why Ruth looked dreadfully tawdry nobody more so than her boyfriend Merimba, he only could dare hope to annihilate all looming yearnings to follow after her father and mother. Full pardon came amending relations between two enigmatic old fond friends. Ruth Eshuba pardoned all guilt in Merimba, she allowed friendship slowly to mature dynamically again.

Goola poached all amenities sprouting yams, old land amounting practically poor livelihood to Merimba, allowed pesetas to Goola from the sale of yams. Goola mapped moles knolls and allowed males for mating to go free, all other females were set free too. The remaining moles fetched lots of money for Goola, as their pelts were much demanded in Parisian fashion houses. Lots of money meant lots of problems, for drink was poor Goola's damnation. All his earnings bought bottle upon bottle of galvanizing drunkness. How a man remained alive, living a lonely gambling with alcoholism life, posed a yearning wish to help in Ruth's heart.

Ruth Eshuba all sad lopped alot of drooping branches from a rose tree in front of her comfortable country cottage. Man certainly comes close to God while working with nature so lovely she seered. Ruth took joy no longer in gardening, but already dolorous thinking was losing ground and fresh happiness had begun dexterously, silently, peacefully, ominously to solve her problem. As she worked she heard Merimba's fast car draw to a lightening halt, he climbed all hurriedly over the fence and lovingly, ceremoniously came towards Ruth. Embracing Ruth he declared his special devotion and there in that idyllic setting he persuaded Ruth to marry him. Though Merimba meant every thing to Ruth, she ignored an early all serious marriage. Calmly she went to Mesazem to work in the old parents' beautiful Pastry Shop. Merimba, an architect and artist by profession, very dejuvenated, smoked a great deal and dreamed his life away.

As some accounts yielded, the forlorn lame mad man lost his life going to Mesazem to Ruth's Pastry Shop to collect a supply of grand homemade bread. Goola Demara found sure kind friendship during long all gadabout tame months, through his friend Ruth.

A door closed peacefully that Saturday in Ruth's shop, she came from the drowning with lovely smells kitchen to serve her next customer. Merimba looked very handsome in his linen suit, the brashness of the blue summer shade heightened the lovely golden hue of his skin. "Some lofty prize or made it yourself?" asked worshipping Ruth. Looking along the pastries slowly, Merimba annoyed Ruth by ignoring completely her happy compliment. He annoyed her still more by demanding fresh pastries, giving a curt nod, and walking purposefully out the door.

Merimba smiled ominously, harshly, suavely as he made his way back to his car. Most nights Ruth drove home on highway one but on Saturday she was in a mixed-up demoralized, despairing state, which made her nervous, she chose to take the lonesome road to Mullaserra. Already it was dark and awful windy when Ruth made her way to her car. As parking remained a problem Ruth arrived long after dark, sad, razor-sharp tired and weary at the motor car park.

Merimba Perangamo, madness forgotten arrived at Ruth's house only to find the door locked. Almost immediately Ruth arrived on the scene, driving very ferocious. Passion obliterated, Merimba nolonger teased Ruth, love appeared strong as he kissed his lovely listless fiancée. Amendment and poor lonely Ruth ameliorated had Merimba feeling on top of the world as he looked back towards Ruth's house on his parting for home.

Ruth Eshuba appeared dashing all hurriedly from her lovely quaint cottage. The rain which never seems to head towards ever hot and drought-filled Egypt, pitter pattered on Ruth's car roof as she landed at pitiful Goola's hovel. Knocking loudly, good friend that she remained always, she looked through the open window to see if Goola's poor wife slovenly lay asleep. A sordid silence saluted her as she opened the door and sadly left honey and bread on the dirty table.

Merimba all separate, lay on his bed thinking about Ruth, all alone, easily awakened, appealing pitifully, longingly for her mother. Pain seemed ever eating into her conscience as she muttered and moaned in her boiling, golden, stuttering voice. Past sweet memories came dearly crowding back into Merimba's fond thoughts, he remembered the first time he met Ruth, it was a glorious great morning, birds sang sweetly, shrilly in the huge garden at the front of Ruth's cottage. As he drew near the front door he found Ruth sowing flowers in ground looking freshly dug. All sweetness came into her certain smile when she greeted him, guiding him into the house she set off serenely to fetch her father. They all then discussed the painting Merimba was planning to do of the homely cottage

Merimba Perangamo lost no time in asking Ruth for a date. From that fond first meeting dear love developed earnestly, gloriously between them.

Damp ground good earth makes, thought Bakara Monat as drops dampened arid dry loamy clay on the fallow, all beautiful, marvellous loud land of the Nile River Valley. All lovely weather past years had found undermines poor idle people's livelihood. Forlorn, god-forsaken peoples ferreted a scanty existence under dreadful raging sun, as millions of gallons of delicious cool, clear water lapped wastefully on. People rose altogether to allow the easelbalast roar of the water to be used to irrigate enlarged lots, allotting loose, God's dewy pearldrops on the lassitral humid land.

Merimba Perangamo allowed people to tell him their gremlin-gullible, hot lurid loose jokes, but inwardly he was a man aware of sad solace for responsible human effort in the salvation of lotments of special, all electric powered irrigated land from which lovely labyrinthian loquacious peoples could manage to thrive upon.

Ruth Eshuba prayed lowly, earnestly, pitiably, sadly as she fought frightfully for her life, low tolls to pay if death could be averted. Food was being fed intravenously, putting new life into flagging low determination. Ruth passed all delirious deafening growling hours each day in lonely, gazing, all anxious silence.

Goola Demara peered poorly towards the approaching cellar, towards easy all acute oblivion. He always spoke sweetly, respectfully to Ruth but that changed woefully the windy night when Ruth put her foot down and refused to let him get into her grey crowded car. Each fresh cake that rested on the car seat was for customers of Ruth and had to be delivered to their homes. Goola always relied on Ruth giving him lifts so when he stopped her car that night and he was refused, he became very angry, insanely angry. Putting the accelerator violently down Ruth darted forward striking Goola who had gun-shotted himself in front of the moving car. The car furiously crossed the boisterous, daring, lumbering, human remains of Goola Demara and finished up lying on its roof on ground fouled up by leaking, lurid, disgusting sewer pipes. Poor Ruth lay on lonely soggy stinking ground all injured and unconscious, pastries and smashed cakes loose on top of her.

Bakara Monat brought the sad news to his fond munificent friend Merimba Perangamo. Through lonely years he had told Bakara he would stand by him until river water made viable his poor plot of land.

Merimba accepted the hospital's hopeless verdict with unusual calmness. Losing no time he made beautiful plans for his marriage to Ruth.

Bells pealed, candles burned, priest's blessings given, smiling tear-stained faces turned to watch Merimba wheel his wife, Ruth Perangamo into love and life.

11 February – 18 March 1978

Her Horse

A short story for 8 to 10 year olds

Early one morning on a Friday always to be remembered, as
Polly made an applepie in her electric cooker she forgot to switch
on the heat to the oven. Rain in foolish loud splashing belted
alarmingly against the dark window. Dull ladders of light
entered through unopened curtains allowing Polly to turn out
the light. Hot porridge made golden pools under creamy milk
on the newly laid table.

Mounting her horse Yes, slowly, dreamily, happily she can-
tered down under tall gagegreen trees to lose her cap on the
marsh. The rain made little rivulets of water pour annoyingly,
speedily, leeringly down Polly's honest face all while she
searched for her cap. Yes ate lovely green grass rapidly, relishing
getting time to graze peacefully.

Polly Earley meanwhile met all calamities with a resolve meant
to amend good loving pleasurable friendships. Polly, young
though she was, lonely, lost and without a boy to say "spoil-
sport" always pulled laughing naughty airs once her appearance
got mentioned. Men all loved Polly's manner and horses loved
it too.

Yes loved her lovely mannered mistress and all horses envied
her. Manly oatbags hung on and held secure by a strap, allowed
Yes to eat her oats. An east wind blew across the stable door as
Yes chewed and enjoyed her breakfast. Hot air lovingly blew
through vents in the stable walls and dried Yes's muck-splattered
coat.

Polly Earley munched greedily on hot buttered toast, looking
usually spoilt she would take less to eat than anyone else in her
family. Moss Musgrave munched lovingly on his toast and
heaped plenty of marmalade onto another slice. Morning passed
over. Polly Earley's appearance passing an appletart all white
back into the oven allowed Moss the hidden excuse to pull
Polly's leg.

Moss Musgrave mentioned the modern method of cooking porkpies, "It ought to be greatly welcomed by scattered brain people like you Polly" he said. "It is called a Micro-wave oven" suggested Moss as a long lob of Narcissi stalks curled around his neck, he made a ghastly shudder and made hastily for the door.

Near Polly's house on a farm made pleasant by the moorland looking over to the range of mitre-pointed, purple heather-clothed mountains on the distant horizon, lived Joan Martin. Polly met Joan a long time ago when out riding, it was *Machra Na Feirme meeting night in the Martins' house and Polly mentioned this point to Joan.

Moss Musgrave, Joan Martin and Polly Earley planned a morning meeting on Musgrave's lovely meadow. No men ever accompanied the girls before, so Moss Musgrave looked very happy mounting his horse that Friday.

Mankind guns down much of nature's monstrous non-productive marsupials. Hundreds munch their wonderous way meekly thought Polly as mice made a bolt for the door leaving an oatbag gushing madly through a gnawed gaping hole. Yes made prancing movements as Polly made last minute mute mutations before riding towards Musgrave's meadow.

Joan Martin made every man think a girl Friday was a necessity but Moss Musgrave knew differently. No later than Wednesday last Joan said that Moss never loved anybody but himself and to Moss Musgrave's disgust Polly Earley happened to be listening.

Joan Martin allowed Polly and Moss to lead off on the morning gallop, she fell in behind on her bay mare. Most mornings a full gallop allowed the horses happy exercise, numerous "yeaps" rang-out as Yes beautifully cleared every obsticle. On this Friday morning Polly noticed when she gave Yes her early morning canter that Yes limped ever so slightly. On her return to the stable she lovingly lifted her horse's hoof and scraped out dead leaves and clay. Now on Yes and galloping hard, Polly noticed Moss Musgrave pointing across towards Goder Hill.

* Machra Na Feirme – from the gaelic – Young Farmers Association.

Joan Martin always loved Goder Hill, every chance she got meant a gallop to a secret hideaway, dark and peaceful, perched on top of the lovely hill. Polly visited the Goder, loving the serenity and nouances, donning hoards secretly accumulated down the centuries.

Moss Musgrave merely lamented tarnishing his noble horse's hooves, making him scramble and slide on the sharp incline. He only gave thought to the much more important company along side him. Moss and Polly and Joan eventually rode abreast, as the ground got more muddy they reined-back their horses to a trot. Moaning now and then Yes made last lame steps before meekly falling and floundering on the muddy ground. Poor Polly leaped glumly from her lifeless horse, a dreadful deathly pallor spreading over her lonely face. Moss immediately sprang into action, "Joan" he said "hold the horses" and mollifying Polly he led her away.

When all post-mortem examinations were completed the findings revealed that Yes's death resulted from severe heart failure.

The End

29 March – May 1978

Writings

Age 13 Years

Through his typewriter Christy gained release from his tongue-tied world. Now, he set his sights on the next hurdle, a breakthrough into the world of normal, full-time education at an ordinary secondary school. Success did not come easily. Time and time again he was made to experience absolute despair as one particular school rejected our every approach. Therefore when acceptance and admission to Mount Temple Comprehensive School came, it brought with it an added bonus, it restored Christy's faith in himself.

Mount Temple, with a student population of almost eight hundred took him to their hearts and with encouragement from an especially enlightened teaching staff and with unobtrusive though caring help from his classmates in 1L he felt himself eased into the everyday life of the school.

Long schooldays sapped his energy, but nonetheless he somehow managed to mark his thirteenth year by writing his first play.

Bernadette Nolan

Water?

All mountain,
All sloppy hulk,
All pouring plural,
All maw, all material
To annex to sea.

At break to block,
To cascade, to glow
To ceding, allowing moot.
Tabby, all phosphorescent,
Wan womb, all aqua,
At christening all queenly.

10 February 1979

The Green Environment

Among firs, a cone high-flown,
Winged, popped,
Hied, foraying, embalming,
Sembling tomb
Among coy, conged fir needles,
A migratory off-spring
Embarks on life's green film.

2 April 1979

Maybe?

Orders of parents heedlessly heard,
Orders of clergy leeringly jeered,
Orders of teachers mimicked and chuckled,
Orders of ruffians menacingly buckled.
Orders on mugging and knifing your foes
Ominously occur on family video shows,
Orders old folk always laced with love,
Orders only earthly topic, obtainable – maybe?

8 April 1979

Inimitable Christopher

Christopher Columbus made man pine,
Natural bounderies wither in continents quest,
With limitless intrigue, in mind boggling timing,
His Nina, his Pinta and his Santa Maria
Gave Isabella a frontier
On a mighty New World.

29 April 1979

Corpus Christi

Icons offering authority,
Quiet Aves all powerfully affording
To Christ's life on cameo portrayed,
Invocation, pollination and immolation.

Mankind – God's people – His Church,
Corpus Christi avowing Heaven's pledge,
Anointing Excelsior's Offering,
In His Last Supper of love.

5 June 1979

The Dignity of Man

Would poor eclecticism, baby
Male, midwife, walk, toddle,
For livelihood, he potters.
Mows-off threats, looks life
In repining, alone he aestivates,
Notable sometimes, dignity of man.

Nothing molests mankind anecdotal,
Women to pillage, recollection
Of Mary, loved and glorified.
Poorly man stumbles, poorly
Man hungers, lovingly offers
God's dignity to man.

23 August 1979

Lovely Fortune?

Time looks back on life,
Lived in noiseless isolations,
Lonely lines of life,
All babbling baby damnations.

Moving narrow limbs,
In constant dire limitations,
Frightening simple friends
With molesting alienations.

Nothing ameliorated matters,
All parents lived their loss,
Watching holiness in invocation
As their child carried his cross

Earlier maddening knolls
Rang nought in inspiration,
Maledictions leaned menacingly
On every annihilation

Loving clouds of welcome
Managed to invent an ideation.
Whither on gossamer wings
Animated an animal mentation

Looks of poor mollification,
Schooled lonely lovely dreams,
Toils looked down on holy happenings
Accruing intriguing wrenching seams.

In seams of mintgreen milling,
Eulogies came and went,
In lovely schools of muses
Vibrated his arresting bent.

Normal-life went on about him,
Nourishing his sullen soul,
Immolating all illusions,
Icing hard his incredible goal.

Immediate jarring jollifications,
In elating wasting looks,
Wondering havens of innate intuition
Illuminated all indeterminate nooks.

Mingling music with perseverance,
Mingling molesting inveigling quells,
In looming life-long lessons
Quietness came in typing spells.

Ivory, foreign, independent mitres
Capped all God-given skills,
Inconsequential looked golden holly
As it prickled with many ills.

The above poem gives a peep into the mind of the totally paralysed, speechless
person who in order to maintain sanity, lives in communion with God and with
his own mind's musical musings.

28 August 1979

Pontiff Poet

Among officials Pope John Paul towers,
Vatican city offers illustry to ours,
Irish ill-feelings are looking dour,
Intruding lovelessly in Ireland's Hour.

Pope John Paul's life leaves sane men hope,
Making non-pilgrims notice how not to mope,
Hell-fire's timeworn missive rings true,
Inviting hibernating catholics to start anew.

Ireland meanwhile makes marvellous plans,
From all corners of the isle she rallies her clans,
Fiercely intruding on people's slumberings,
Churchbells will ring-out with almighty thunderings.

Nothing needlessly mutters nigh listen,
Nothing all baneful need cloud true christian,
Nothing magical can move the soul,
Peace casts its eye, will you be its goal?

Ireland, may your fathers' glorious faith,
Languish garnered in veritable fruitful state,
Nobody pours peaceful apostolic prayer,
Silence, solemnly give Pope John Paul a care.

11 September 1979

Low Ceiling

This play is set in dreary crowded wetday Dublin.

THOMAS HAND a teacher; EITHNE BOURKE a hotel waitress and Thomas Hand's girlfriend; AVRIL NOLAN a dressdesigner; OLIVER NOLAN is an aeroplane pilot and is Avril's husband; JOHN NOLAN is their son and is a student; MR. DEVINE the school principal.

ACT I   Scene 1

In school principal's office.

THOMAS HAND	All bloody hell has broken out here to-day Eithne, and small wonder when his table offered neighing idling callous brats ammunition to fight with.
EITHNE	Was your can of beauties involved?
THOMAS	No, as luck would have it they were playing an inter schools basketball match.
EITHNE, *slowly sipping coffee*	Was the principal's table valuable, or was it the principle of the thing?
THOMAS	Damn you and your false puns, the murderous curs savaged a beautiful antique sable coloured mahogany table presented to the founder on his school's Silver Jubilee in 1914.
EITHNE	I didn't mean to be funny Tom, but I couldn't resist asking the question. Seriously though, what can be done – dare one give the school a bad name by calling in the fuzz?

THOMAS, *collecting the empty coffee cups and carelessly planting a dour kiss on Eithne's cheek*	Nasty bastards all cops, I look on them as vermin – awkward arrogant upstarts.
EITHNE, *making an ugly face*	Remember numb-skull now you're taking my father's name into disrepute.
THOMAS, *unrepentant*	I don't see how your father brought himself to fasten that uniform on him and he federal minded like me.
EITHNE, *sternly sadly frowning*	As you're so federal minded why don't you vacillate respect where your country's hugely jested defence forces are concerned?
THOMAS, *knife-like fending off attacks*	The dander is up in me since police towed away my car to the pound and damn fool that I am, I had to pay £5.00 to redeem it. Damn blast sanity, police give me a pain ever since.
EITHNE, *biting her spoon*	Come-on moron, as you lack sanity on direction of the hands of time, I may as well tell you that you have a class in five minutes.
THOMAS, *looking flustered*	Do you know, only for my breathing sane watch I would have forgotten all about it.

Taking the cups they hurriedly hug each other and leave the office.

Scene 2
In the foyer of Dublin Airport.

Avril Nolan sits smoking nervously as Oliver's plane touches down. He steps into the Arrivals Lounge and glances all around.

AVRIL, *rushing towards him, kisses him*

Darling you're more than welcome, come with me to the bar and we'll have a quick drink – our love and faith in John, our darling dashing son looks like crashing all about our ears.

OLIVER, *frowning greatly heads off to the bar and orders their favourite drinks – kindly turning to his wife*

Please save me from going mad by telling me what all this bull is all about.

AVRIL, *taking a careful sip of her drink*

You know how dependable John always was, well seemingly the devil got into him lately and hell hath no fury like our son as he led a gang on a rampage in The Founder's Lounge in school yesterday.

OLIVER, *looking aghast*

Our John wouldn't do anything ghastly like that.

AVRIL

Save your breath darling there is worse to come. Yesterday the phone rang, it was Mr. Devine, the school principal. He wanted to speak to you. I explained that you were travelling back to-day from Chicago on this flight. He said could you come straight away, as your son John seems to be in terrible trouble, I enquired lifelessly if he had had an accident – Mr. Devine reassured me but gave me to understand that the case in question was urgent and grave.

OLIVER, *all ghastly and agitated*

Galling bastard, trying to involve an absolutely innocent boy in some escapade of his damned demented school.

AVRIL, *rattily*

Parents are suckers to believe their offspring are celestial beings bestowed with all gracious god-like characters, when in fact all children, including our angel scare the daylights out of baulked bold brats.

OLIVER, *annoyed with Avril*

Can't you come clean now and for God's sake say what happened.

AVRIL, *ponderously*

Yesterday was just like to-day, lashing lousy rain fell non-stop. Last bell of the morning peeled out in school. All classes went to lunch. Several classes opted to go to the gym for a basketball match. Where damned fifth years got the cider and aspirin is not yet established, but they drank themselves stupid down in the tennis pavilion. The after lunch bell rang at 2 o'clock and ten fifth years failed to turn up for Art Class, among them our White Hope.

OLIVER, *meanly mad, eyes bulging*

God. I'll kill him, I'll kill him.

AVRIL, *slowly*
purposefully   At around five o'clock the denigration of
the beautiful antique furniture and price-
less objets d'art took place. The Founder's
Lounge was a sorry looking sight. Every-
thing was smashed and on the artfully de-
signed low ceiling, yes, you've guessed it,
were executed the most daring disgusting
suggestive caricatures imaginable.

With tears of shame flowing down their faces...

OLIVER, *taking*
his wife's hand   Let's get out of here.

They walk embarrassedly towards the door.

Scene 3

Nolans' kitchen. John Nolan sitting recalcitrantly watching tele-
vision. In storms his sad looking Mam and his damned-angry
Dad.

OLIVER,
powerfully afraid
of his own temper   Go switch off the TV, we have more tor-
rid, turbulent things to discuss.

John slowly, deftly switches on to other channels before finally
switching off the set.

OLIVER, *noticing*
the dalliance in
his son's defiance   Look smart cur and feverishly give an
honest account of your activities in school
yesterday.

JOHN, *slowly*
turning to
scathingly smile
at his dad   Haven't teachers always sinned in their

handling of youth. From time immemorial
to this present day teachers have quoted
saws excusing youthfull excavations in
scholarly lofty plains of truth. Afraid
of questions, teachers astutely branded
youths with enquiring, curious minds as
trouble-makers and cowards – cowards
who always backed-down without finding
answers. Cut down solely, fiercely again
and again built acute frustration and re-
sentment in me.

OLIVER, *spoiling
John's manly
longings to
account for his
actions*   Pagan affrontry bodes ill minds.

JOHN, *losing the
argument's sway*   Christ dad, can you not spare me the time
                                 either to talk – of course you never did,
                                 casual asceticism was always your answer
                                 to my poor primitive probing.

OLIVER, *leaning
back far and
assuming a snide
nonchalance*   Bad luck always rears its snarling snout
                                 under accounts of mating Godgiven in-
                                 quisitiveness with manmade metering of
                                 dammed, exquisite information.

AVRIL, *sitting
quietly, erratically
speaks*   Please wait until you have heard all of
                                 John's story before commenting Oliver.

OLIVER, *angrily*   Look sharp boy.

JOHN, *feeding daggers looks to his dad*	Ostensibly strife-torn order nurses vandalism. Among cankerous capons, all mindful lads cannot blandly feign alarm, placating especially modes of conformation, established all hiddenly by wilful wreckers of social order.
OLIVER, *all maligned, bites back an angry reply – patiently*	John, are you napcapping in the doldrums of schoolboy listlessness?
JOHN	Most timid boys losing time coping elatingly, tacitly with lonesome love's call conspicuously masquerade their dashing, growing dolorous drives.
OLIVER	Pegasus' lasting beauty sallies on to assure the fallopian tubes access all lovely through acorns all venereally sacrileged.
JOHN *coyly answers*	Lonely mesmerism longs furiously for on-the-spot answers.
OLIVER, *annoyed, calls all his annihilating plethora of pleadings*	Omar Khayyam always wanted to loosely lose himself in pondering poorly on the pleasure of love.
JOHN, *very bashful*	Mam and Dad, can ye see what I'm trying to say, at the back of all my odious philanderings I'm sure mixed-up.

AVRIL, *mediating*   Oliver, nagging checks flows of sanity. Lonely snatching of Roman god-like rendezvous sadly appals mammalians.

JOHN, *not mincing words*   Sap, boys in school imitate teaching, affiliating lonely polar-cool hopes with day-long, spurs-sharp rejection.

OLIVER *peacefully asks*   Avril, can you make a pot of strong tea? Perhaps all parties will see sense then.

AVRIL   Would both of you go into the lounge and I'll make the tea.

The men leave the kitchen as Avril goes towards the kettle.

ACT II   Scene 1

In Avril's 'Hits From Minstrels' Boutique.

EITHNE, *lost in peaceful passivity, thumbs doll-like dresses on the pages of Avril's ledger*   All appearances lose glaring blemishes placed alluringly within 'Hits From Minstrels' creations. Thomas!

THOMAS, *smartalecky, vehemently parries*   Poor Avril is germinating last-ditch, sly sketches trying to come up with something to grace all the imperfections in Eithne Bourke's physique.

EITHNE, *making awful galling faces*	Would you shut-up, always yapping, as if you could afford to talk!
THOMAS *publicly sports a kiss on Eithne's cheek*	Sorry love, I'll mend my manners.
EITHNE, *fashioning material over her shoulders*	Allow me to get on with my marriage plans.
THOMAS, *lassooing Eithne with the muslin-like material*	As you don't want my expert opinion I may as well vamoose.
AVRIL, *carrying along a cape of satin*	Goodbye Thomas, a man may never be allowed to see his love's bridal attire.

Smiling broadly Thomas goes out the door.

EITHNE, *looking excitedly at the bottle-shaped cape*	I'm mad anxious to see your loveliest bridal creation.
AVRIL, *mysteriously opens the cape*	Pals usually know each other's tastes.
EITHNE, *loudly gasping*	Avril, as pagan poets sometimes said "Golden Moguls almost wonder". Lovely, perfect, adorable – Avril you're a wizard at materializing dreams.

AVRIL, *saying very matter-of-factly*	Hits are my speciality!
EITHNE *all trembling with anticipation*	Please help me slip the dress over my head, I'm nervously all fingers and might rip some of this beautiful lace.
AVRIL, *lifting the lace frock slips it over Eithne's head*	Grip it feebly and slip it down gently, this does seem to answer your measurements perfectly. Now - I'll close the zip.
EITHNE *silently dreamily inspects her reflection in the mirror*	Oh Avril really it's beautiful, I am pleased beyond words.
AVRIL, *all pleased*	Pleating non-pressed, gives a nice effect and makes the skirt move lovely.
EITHNE, *very happy*	In acclaiming such magnificent lace I now would dare ask the price of my dear frock?
AVRIL *ponders*	One hundred pounds on materials – the design and time spent creating it are on me.
EITHNE, *numbed by Avril's generous pulverising offer*	Owning a magically imaginative boutique must bring immense profits but also immense company overheads. I want to really take all that into account when allowing joint exclusiveness in your design and for-

	feiting true monetary tone in making up my bill.
AVRIL *loses the trend of Eithne's thinking*	Delight in a satisfied client's outpourings means more sometimes than cold cash.
EITHNE, *looking thoughtful*	Please mention money for work par excellence Avril.
AVRIL, *frowning greatly*	Perhaps you would give me £20.00 for my slightly skilful design and we'll both be pleased.
EITHNE, *moved very much*	Lasting sure friends look like becoming lovely life-long losers.
AVRIL, *laughing noisily*	Come-on Eithne, heave yourself out of your frock and for heaven's sake don't tear it.

Laughing happily they begin to undo the zip.

ACT II   Scene 2

In school principal's office.

MR. DEVINE, *sporting a sparse beard, looks up through nail-cuticled bi-focals at Oliver, Avril and John Nolan*	Please take a seat – it's terrible queer to find John Nolan in this situation. Mindful of

your longstanding role all kindness will be brought to bear to fathom your reasons John for wantonly carrying out this foolhardy jaunt.

Smiling lightly, gaining another sane moment's respite, John cloaks saucy waspish words.

JOHN, *rising to his feet*

Mr. Devine, Mam, Dad, John Nolan, naive though he may be asks all of you to obliterate langetting sconced happenings in school, and smash cold memories as well, beautifying fresh creativity, as dolefully I vow, to more than make loneliness nash jasmine-sweet fads in blithe, fond, lovable amends.

OLIVER, *looking at Mr. Devine, lays a blunt blank cheque on the principal's desk*

May I spool all our poor son's usage of valiant, loud, looming lawdidaw regrets and on behalf of his mother and myself please fill-in the hundreds necessary to pick-up the maddening remains.

MR. DEVINE, *putting the blank cheque in his safe, turns to the three gloomy people*

We'll fittingly have the damage assessed by experts and you may be sure we will always make a sane attempt to make things camouflage the awful heartache involved for John.

JOHN, *moved bashfully cries lonesome tears*

Mr. Devine, please forgive my nonsensical behaviour, moreover, can you befriend me enough to be very sure I will bring delicate glory as I represent your school in days hence.

MR. DEVINE *very politely moves towards John and tapping him over the head with his hand*

Well John, I naturally feel dashed sorry for myself but naturally I also have deep sympathy for you and your wonderful, loyal parents. Despite what has happened you will be welcome to carry-on your studies here.

AVRIL *and* OLIVER, *blocking each other in excitement*

Oh! Mr. Devine, our son owes you great thanks. *(Avril's voice)* ... I can't believe you'll let John by. *(Oliver's voice)*

JOHN, *falsely starting to fasten-on his delighted sentiments*

All my thanks goes lovingly to all three of you.

MR. DEVINE *moves to open the door*

How about a cup of tea? – come along with me, we could all do with a cup.

All four of them leave the office   John closing the door

ACT II   *Final Scene*

In Hotel Montague Dining Room.
Bridal group seated at long main table.

Bestman JOHN
NOLAN *rises for
the last time and
calls*

Attention please, I just want to ask you all
to excuse Tom and Eithne – let fashion's
flashiest model get easy relief from looking
lovely as she changes from regal white into
her going-away suit.

Tom and Eithne leave the nuptial feast to loud applause.

In the bar later on the same day.

MR. DEVINE,
*non-plussed by
John's
performance
during the long
day*

All I modestly do say is, John Nolan, please
accept very sincere congratulations on the
magnificent way you carried out your
responsibilities to-day. About what hap-
pened in Mount Vernon, could we pretend
this episode never occurred, madness with
man's ironing-flat of youth's pursuit of
poise, through freedom to quest hell-
fogged knowledge, very ichorously nour-
ishes vandalism.

AVRIL, *moving
nimbly, orders
John not to forget
his duties towards
Thomas*

Boy, don't number yourself free until your
friend Thomas and his bride get away first.

MR. DEVINE,
*gallantly ushers
John along*

Look out for me John, I have a wee job to
do on a very special car.

Mr. Devine hurries happily away.

OLIVER,
*searching for Mr.
Devine*

For heaven's sake John, did you see your
head-master anywhere, he asked me to
help him do a job on Thomas Hand's car.

JOHN, *looking for
any sign of
Thomas*

Dad, look outside, don't you know where
Thomas parked his car last night.

JOHN, *seeing a lot
of fuss at the dark
end of the stairs
gets his guests
assembled*

Attention everybody, here comes Mr. and
Mrs. Thomas Hand.

There is loud cheering, whistling and plodding applause.

EITHNE, *standing
smiling broadly
on the bottom
step of the stairs*

GIRLS, GIRLS, come and catch my bouquet.

*A charge forward of smiling giggling girls jump to catch the
lovely pink and white roses.*

THOMAS, *glancing*
away sees
confetti-trouble
approaching,
grasping Eithne
by the hand   Quick love, let's get out of here, there's a
                       possie after us...

Laughing nervously, they run towards the door as all of the
guests run after them.

                    The curtain falls.

                        23 May – 13 December 1979

Writings

Age 14 Years

Almost all of Christy's writings are meant to give aural pleasure. I discovered that truth each time he begged me to read over and over again the sentence which he had just typed, whilst he sat, head averted, listening intently to the sounds and effects of his words.

As well as experimenting with his art, Christy now had to do battle with newfound notoriety. His prize-winning entry in The Spastics Society's Literary Contest coupled with Edna Healey's heralding of his apparent genius, sent the BBC and The Sunday Times hurrying to his doorstep. BBC Radio gave an airing to his poetry while The Sunday Times Colour Magazine, published a story about him accompanied by superbly taken Snowdon photographs.

Following on this expansive publicity came new hope flashing on and off on the horizon, as interested people advanced theories of how Christy's method of writing could be speeded-up. One particular phone-call though caught our special attention. It came from Phil Odor, a Research Fellow at Edinburgh University. His theory held the promise that in years to come his research would eventually lead Christy to an independent form of self-expression, hitherto undreamed of.

This hectic life with all its new challenges left Christy feeling fatigued. A holiday was planned on the Dingle Peninsula of Co. Kerry, but the peaceful scenery there which poured balm on the tired spirits of the family, served but to act as a stimulus to Christy's imagination. He was even anxious for the holiday to end in order to return to his new computer and through it to empty-out his mental store of Kerry-inspired poetry. Relief for him came on 28 August and he worked non-stop for fourteen hours writing a series of short poems.

Bernadette Nolan

Nobody

A play for television

This rollicking, maddeningly provocative play is set in Dingle – a beautiful fishing village in Co. Kerry, Ireland.

CHRISTOPHER BALL, a weasel-sad, lost ex-priest; BERNADETTE MARTIN, friend; DANIEL O'CONNELL, the owner of Dally-a-while Caravan Site; PHELIM O'NEILL, a visiting trainee priest.

ACT I

Tokens of joisting summer breezes mingle mournfully, spooning pleasure into the Dingle Peninsula. Smoking all peacefully, Christopher Ball seated on the steps of his Irish horse-drawn caravan, listens thoughtfully as Phelim O'Neill's plaintive playing of Danny Boy on the Uileann Pipes drifts darkly through the cadences of his mind.

CHRISTOPHER BALL, *lost in lonesome adjustments, looks slowly at Phelim as he finishes playing*

My best thanks to you Phelim for bringing nature's lovely hauntings leaping into my madness-tethered soul.

PHELIM O'NEILL, *a huskiness coming sensitively into his voice*

A man certainly can scrape momentary freedom from despair, as he nods acquaintance with the musical mastery of the muses.

CHRISTOPHER, *all
numbed by sad
feelings*
                    Dastardly slow nuances conjure mighty
                    lovely depths, laid low in resonance.

PHELIM, *moving
naturally man-
sized buttocks on
a fashionable
low-life lycra
motor-bike jacket*
                    All vexed questions a fierce agile charis-
                    matic mind concocts can be accommo-
                    dated within the realms of music.

CHRISTOPHER,
*noticing nothing
nonsensical in
Phelim's lunges
into plethoras of
learned logic*
                    Life normally allows music-allotment's
                    anointing balm access all lovely to
                    universal, undulating man.

PHELIM, *nicely
freed, fetters
panniers
musically into
place, treading
much grass as
sadly he prepares
his bike for
departure*
                    Vegetable green gives me about as much a
                    reminder of lonesome longings as Danny
                    Boy venially tumbles you into announce-
                    ments of musical importunity.

CHRISTOPHER,
*blinking moist
eyes*
                    Nobody ever knows feelings of pain without

also loitering sometimes, in the realms of apparent azure blue aloe happiness.

PHELIM, *poorly, meekly angles heedlessly*

Given man's munificence in natal, quasi-luminary questioning, ceilings identical ambitions in moaning man's heartfelt meanderings in noble Nemesis.

CHRISTOPHER, *smoking positively*

My mind mellows beautifully, mystically, memorizing naturally noble Nemesis' meaning for human beings.

PHELIM, *identifying church teachings, looks searchingly*

Looming madness menacingly threatens.

CHRISTOPHER, *looking for his penknife, searches each of his pockets – then looks on the ground – not finding it he stands up, climbs the steps and enters the caravan*

I can't find my penknife, you didn't see it anywhere Phelim?

PHELIM, *putting-up a show at searching*

No, no sign of it anywhere.

CHRISTOPHER *loudly calls*

Come in Phelim and I'll make some supper

– you have an early rising in the morning. We can continue mingling logic with life as we eat something.

PHELIM, *dashing up the steps*

I am absolutely starving, my eyes think they will never see food again!

CHRISTOPHER, *lighting gas under the kettle*

Would you like some tomato sandwiches? – mine are special, even if I say so myself.

PHELIM, *looking in the cupboard*

Do you use margarine?

CHRISTOPHER, *looking aghast*

I wouldn't insult my tomato sandwiches.

PHELIM *watches as the kettle boils and moves to make the tea*

I would like to go into a more serious discussion of Nemesis and the more obvious insights to be found in the philosophy of life.

CHRISTOPHER, *biting deeply into a sandwich*

My mind casually denies treasured dandied doctrines flouting dastardly heinous municipal Nemesis as magical mead dosed out to each one of us.

PHELIM, *pouring tea*

The main difference between you and me is not mundane philosophy but a mystical faith on my part and absolute agnosticism on yours.

CHRISTOPHER,
*munching
thoughtfully*

Nobody can prove the existence of God, most of all altruistic Man.

PHELIM, *moving
his mug and plate*

Among notable mullings on this yearnful, notoriously lonely question, I read somewhere that sinful man's greatest obsticle to belief is his complete neurotic naïveté.

CHRISTOPHER, *no
longer interested
in church, knives
God-illusions
ferociously*

Man's materializing mental alertness must manufacture numerous, cold, tantalizing, logic-locked, labyrinthian perplexities, as he delves deeply in hopeless questings.

PHELIM, *sanguine,
notes his friend's
bunglings*

Lonely sentinels in the theology of Theism make lousy leaps in text-book lore.

CHRISTOPHER,
*numbed by
Phelim's
vociferous defence
immediately
declares*

Venial nude mullings gild much vehement priggish belief, ousting vital looming nebulae of innovation.

PHELIM, *between
two minds speaks
slowly*

Maybe innovations might bring bastions tumbling down mummifying a lovely customary christian heritage.

CHRISTOPHER,
*freed as trembling
denial frees*   Can mighty man venture into life in pursuit
                                 of happiness?

PHELIM *nudges
cups in a few
inches from the
edge of the table*   More and more onerous new nomadic
                                 muniments move luminously across
                                 youth's-land, messing pastures munifi-
                                 cently sowed with the grain of purity and
                                 truth.

CHRISTOPHER,
*venially all thumbs,
natters moodily*   Among much nubile awakenings nine out
                                 of ten women mention marriage to an ex-
                                 priest as tantamount to nullity.

PHELIM, *narrowly
missing knocking
numerous
precepts of
religious belief*   Wildly may I wonder who you have in
                                 mind when you announce marriage wor-
                                 ries.

CHRISTOPHER,
answering meekly   My long time lovely friend is Bernadette
                                 Martin, she is the widow of my great friend
                                 Ned who died tragically four years ago.

PHELIM, *noticing
how interested his
friend seemed in
Bernadette*   My sympathies now lie with Bernadette
                                 and her moronic attachment to you.

CHRISTOPHER,
much amused,
moves
momentarily to
nurse his
embarrassment
I mention my old friend in order to explain why I'm interested.

PHELIM, *noticing*
much involvement
in Christopher's
lively fussings
Jests – always breathe rash ridicule into older men's mention of love.

CHRISTOPHER,
numbed by
Phelim's
observations,
obeys life's call to
respond lashingly
Mastering irate madness wears savagely on the nerves.

PHELIM, *dumbed*
bluntly, makes
drumming noises
with his fingers
on the table
Lubricating lopsided logic leans loomingly low in men's minds.

CHRISTOPHER,
nastily angry,
merely mumbles
Venting nubile notions negates much munificent nominal christianity.

PHELIM, *nettled*
needlessly
Benedictions wedded to Bernadette baffles much nuptial balmy bliss.

CHRISTOPHER, *all nasty, looks with contempt at Phelim*	My manhood dream was to nullify my mad desires and devote my mighty nothingness to GOD.
PHELIM, *lonely in his loveless collar-encircled dreams*	Light leads where GOD lovingly beckons.
CHRISTOPHER, *moistening his finger picks up a piece of paper off the floor*	My faith is gone forever.
PHELIM, *meek in his mental submission*	My money is on you finding GOD again in your clerical life.
CHRISTOPHER *mops tears off his face by rubbing with his waistcoat*	Nursing breathing luminous life in murderous manical, negative longing makes man mundane.
PHELIM, *numbed, branches carefully into safer territory*	My nastiness poisoned a very beautiful modest moment in our lives.
CHRISTOPHER *murmurs*	I forgive you.

Phelim steps over to Christopher's chair and reliably placing an arm around his shoulders, roughly hugs a sad friend.

The cameras swing slowly away.

ACT II

This scene is dangerously set. Years ago a zany God, Lusar, made men curse reason. On the Great Skellig, a precipitous rock jutting out of the sea they defied nature. They were followed later by Early Christian Monks who established a settlement there.

DANIEL
O'CONNELL
*cannot be
described –
among men, he
meekly lifted
appearances of
noble manhood*

Ventures such as this make me blazing mad. I'll leave it all to you Bernadette, but remember it's miles out to the Great Skellig.

BERNADETTE
MARTIN, *lovely,
lonely and mild
tempered, moves
all looks of venial
admiration from
love-lorn men
into beautiful
caring candid
concern*

Please make landing arrangements. Nobody ever met their God without nourishing all cellulose medieval lunges into man's justification of heresy of terrible terror.

DANIEL, *heaving a
long sigh,
buttresses heaps*

of timber in his boat, lashing it down well with a strong rope	I don't understand a word you're saying Bernadette. Long winded arguments make me sick – particularly when they attempt to allot intelligence to a mere woman!!
BERNADETTE, *looming nearer nudges Daniel in tomboy style*	Lonely, noticeably attractive women can be passably intelligent as well.
DANIEL *fondly hugs his light-hearted friend*	Get along with yourself now and between us we very likely might drown poor Christopher, as we take-on the Skelligs Rock.
BERNADETTE, *noticeably moist-eyed*	To lessen our life – even by one day, makes me sad.
DANIEL, *looking away worriedly towards the distant rocks*	Nobody can peer into frenzied, life-lonely despair, without considering GOD-defying death.
BERNADETTE, *awfully moved by Daniel's thinking*	Nobody ever notices a man's alertness until it may be too late.

DANIEL *suavely brushes a fleck of dust off his fisherman's style yellow jumper*

Iconoclasts loom into fierce festering laughing-focus, pugilistically popularizing mankind's nomadic, alluring, neurological novelties.

BERNADETTE, *affording certain lovely looks in the direction of the ex-priest's dallient, dead, harness-rattling, horse-hoof beating approach*

Feel free to call Christopher an iconoclast Daniel, better not annoy a poor fellow by letting him hear a label like that being tacked on his character. I cannot for the life of me see where all your bookish-alive, ermine-wrapped philosophy emanates from. Could it be that a plodding, roaming iconoclast got into you, aligning outrageous always, logic's full offensive, mentally neutralizing lofty spirituality.

DANIEL *silently acknowledges much of Bernadette's arguments and averting his able body he merely murmurs*

Ye false Gods. . . .

BERNADETTE, *momentarily numbed, munches nervously on a traithnin**	Nobody nurses grief kindly – but man wins when he does.
DANIEL, *moved weakly, frowns*	I fall-foul of every new loathsome, lewd madcap adventure in theology.
BERNADETTE, *nursing necessary venial meters in her Dominican nuns' education, calms her wind-tossed hair*	Nobody can attempt and want to numb the senses.
DANIEL, *looking towards the caravan site*	Look Bernadette, our friend Christopher has at last arrived.
BERNADETTE, *wooden-faced sets-out to meet an old friend*	You wait down here Daniel, I'll hurry along Christopher.

Leaving Daniel she climbs steps leading from the shore to the caravan site. Christopher Ball seeing Bernadette approaching, stops unyoking his piebald horse and laughingly gives her a fleeting wave. Bernadette, not able to catch her breath, looks smilingly at Christopher as she gently hugs her dear friend.

* Traithnin (pronounced trawneen) the Gaelic word for a hard withered blade of grass.

CHRISTOPHER
nurses a wish to
kiss Bernadette
but gives her a
tender look
instead　　　　　My dearest Bernadette, I never imagined
　　　　　　　　Ballinskelligs meant Paradise. Nobetter
　　　　　　　　place in the world to get sorted out than in
　　　　　　　　this beautiful, munificent, Venice-like gem
　　　　　　　　of creation.

BERNADETTE,
dangling a
medallion with
almost gay
abandon　　　　　My very own Nemesis.

CHRISTOPHER,
bearing down on
her with the horse,
makes as if to
trample on her　　　Run for your life Bernadette.

Christopher lets the mute beast free to graze or tumble in the
green grass.

BERNADETTE,
mumbling
something about
male chauvinist　　　Christopher, lock-up your caravan quickly
　　　　　　　　because Daniel O'Connell pushes-off very
　　　　　　　　soon.

CHRISTOPHER,
nudging his way
into a heavy
sweater makes the
caravan secure　　　How about grub and oil-skins?

BERNADETTE
makes all manner
of questioning
irrelevant   Everything taken care of Sir.

Laughing merrily they set-out down to the shore and Daniel's
boat.

         Later in the same day on the Great Skellig.

The cameras pick-up the scene as Christopher and Bernadette
make ready to have a picnic lunch.

CHRISTOPHER,
much happier in
himself feeds
crusts of bread to
seagulls   I'm very pleased you suggested an outing
to the Great Skellig – the weather is mar-
vellous, and the tea number one.

BERNADETTE,
fearing what she
felt in her bones
Christopher was
about to say only
nibbles on her
sandwich   I'm happy that you like it here.

CHRISTOPHER,
eating ravenously
shoos-off the ever
demanding,
daring seagulls   Get lost seagulls, we may need these sand-
wiches – perhaps we may have to spend
the night here.

BERNADETTE,
*noticing the quip
makes a shudder*

Man dear can you imagine a night spent on a seven hundred foot high rock?

CHRISTOPHER,
looking teasingly

Bernadette dear I can think of worse ordeals.

BERNADETTE,
very embarrassed

Nobody knows the wiles of man but another man.

CHRISTOPHER,
*very non-
committal*

Here is a man who would love you to keep on trying.

BERNADETTE,
*bending down to
hide some of her
embarrassment
picks up an apple
and cleans it with
her serviette*

I think that I know you much better than you know yourself.

CHRISTOPHER
*needlessly
ponders*

Nobetter way to magnify your fanfare of failings than to see yourself through all falsifying rose-coloured spectacles.

BERNADETTE,
*pummelling a
nutbrown
mentally
absorbing
manuscript*

None but the candidly lonely-lettered may attempt to glean comfort all calm from early life's new nefarious nullities.

CHRISTOPHER,
*bending down to
nuisance himself
by lunatically
banging lumps of
rock*

No longer can I mention Bernadette Martin without nursing mundane interest in the kind woman's welfare.

BERNADETTE
*nudges the apple
core into the
ground with a
modicum of
violence*

I am nobody's woman, but I take an interest in you.

CHRISTOPHER
*makes a bold
effort to hide his
feelings, binding a
blade of grass
around his finger*

You know how I worry about you my dear Bernadette. You are always on my mind.

BERNADETTE,
*much moved,
murmurs*

Nobody meekly accepts man's love because love demands sacrifice.

CHRISTOPHER, *no longer knowing how to control manly desires
firmly advances in the direction of his friend. He helps her to
her feet and drawing her scarf tightly around her neck kisses her
on the mouth very passionately.*

BERNADETTE,
*pushing away
Christopher's
arms*

Must you be nolonger aware of your royal

priestly vows which must cling mummify-
ingly mystically to your natural inclina-
tions?

CHRISTOPHER,
not making any
impression on
Bernadette fights
back tears   My dearest Bernadette, my love for you
                                 makes a mockery of my life.

Bernadette now moved to tears walks away and looks out to the
churning sea.

CHRISTOPHER,
wiping away his
nomadic tears
moves to join
Bernadette   My manly desires can no longer do without
                                 a woman and a home of my own.

BERNADETTE,
clears nun-like her
own desires and
gazing at
Christopher   I cannot find feelings in my heart which
                                 may overlook the priestly nonentity in
                                 yours.

CHRISTOPHER,
not meaning to
belittle the
priestly vocation   Nobody can believe unless he is convinced
                                 of the existence of GOD in his heart.

BERNADETTE,
moving away to

*look at the
monastic bee-hive
huts, leads
Christopher by
the hand*

Come and see where our early priests nur-
tured their belief and perhaps you may
once again be revived.

*Christopher, allowing Bernadette to guide him, alertly examines
the poor medieval nuptial of man with* GOD *as evidenced in
anointing workmanship on the 'beehive' cells, the oratories
and the mendicant crosses.*

CHRISTOPHER, *no
longer living in
the present,
moves entirely
openly amazed
eyes*

Nobody may see this munificence of mon-
umental loving nurturing belief and not
notice beautiful schools of thought emerg-
ing out of the sub-conscious.

BERNADETTE, *not
able to fathom the
nurturing inklings
in Christopher's
mind*

Nobody may be numbed by numerical
ecological objectives nolonger maintaining
ameliorating mendicant messages.

CHRISTOPHER,
*not noticing much
encouraging
notions in beastly,
noticeably hellish
nature*

Chronicles can certainly convey more than
crude crosses, but coupled with crude
crosses, Chronicles become codes of celes-
tial certitude.

BERNADETTE, *all poorly heads off towards the picnic remains*

You can follow when you're ready Christopher.

Christopher noting verticals in thinking and churning church teachings now maps mentally a mulling awareness of GOD.

BERNADETTE, *locking-away a beautiful precious moment in her life, looks penchantly moidered as she makes ready for her departure*

Come-on Christopher, you must be quick, Daniel will be waiting for us at the foot of the lighthouse.

Bernadette makes her way towards the stone steps and daringly carrying the picnic basket disappears down the steps. Meanwhile, Christopher, noticing Bernadette's lesson in lovely esoterical caring-devotion, lost in new wonderment he suddenly misses Bernadette and rushing towards the steps he calls GOD, she'll be killed ... Bernadette, Bernadette, *as he gazes anxiously downwards.*

The cameras look downwards too at the churning depths below.

ACT II₁

This Act is once again set on the Dingle Peninsula. Christopher Ball nothing different in appearance, nothing different in behaviour, heads into the Presbytery in Dingle. Stamping out his cigarette butt, vain-like he lengthens his blue sweater and tightening the knot on his mauve tie, he sadly turns the knob on the varnished cedarwood door and quietly enters. Making an almighty noise with the delf Phelim lets a cup fall with fright as he glances round from the sink to greet a visitor ...

PHELIM O'NEILL,
*not able to believe
his eyes*   My moaning jollop, am I seeing things?

Bursting with excitement, he makes a dash for Christopher and hugs him fiercely.

CHRISTOPHER,
*moisteyed, clasps
his friend's
shoulders and
dolefully looking
into his eyes*   Nobody can deny Bernadette Martin's teaching and calming, delightful guidance.

PHELIM, *moved
by Christopher's
nominal, timely,
lonesome
admission*   Nobody would ever deny GOD if they understood mankind's numbing mind.

CHRISTOPHER,
*very happy in
himself*   Nobody vaguely understands where GOD's light brightly beckons.

PHELIM,
*customarily calm
makes every
mealtime error,
letting milk boil
over and the eggs
boil hard*

I don't want to poison you Christopher lad, near thing though it seems to be.

CHRISTOPHER, *in
high spirits,
laughs heartily at
Phelim's messing*

I am unaware of notoriously bad cooking.

PHELIM, *cup of
coffee in hand*

You'll have to agree you have often tasted worse.

CHRISTOPHER,
*casting his down
the sink*

Yes, but one doesn't drink Guinness for breakfast, at least in my days in the seminary we didn't.

PHELIM, *laughing
uproariously*

You were always onto a loser, imagine what each of you missed by not having me around!

CHRISTOPHER
*strikes a punch at
Phelim*

You wouldn't attempt to pawn-off soiled sock water for coffee in my day!

PHELIM, *not in
the least bit
disturbed*

Will you have some tea instead, I can guarantee it.

CHRISTOPHER
*goes over to the
sink and puts on
the kettle*

You can guarantee what – more of the same is it?

PHELIM, *not able to complain sits down and opens an egg*

These will do nicely for salad this evening.

CHRISTOPHER, *rinsing the teapot*

It's breakfast that I'm thinking about.

PHELIM, *much annoyed with himself*

Well for the woman who missed me.

CHRISTOPHER, *moving to put tea in the pot*

Shame on the woman who reared you!

PHELIM, *making much of fetching clean cups*

How can we drink tea made by an expert out of delf cups?!

CHRISTOPHER, *pouring his own brew*

Now, you can drink real tea.

PHELIM, *growing rowdy with impatience*

Now that we have settled the serious matter of making damn tea, may we now discuss the less serious matter of what the hell has you bursting in here and getting me to change my menu.

CHRISTOPHER, *not able to contain his great news*

I have gained a yearning for the Priesthood. GOD certainly brought me back with a vengeance. Bernadette moved my heedless, certified commitment to my calling – she as much as told me that very big callings require very big candid committed men. Phelim, sensitivity to an awareness of joyful knowledge of GOD's beautiful electrifying existence, bellowed numbingly through my nefarious, neap-tide, soulless, nullifying agnosticism.

PHELIM, *overjoyed, lambasts his bearded monk-friend*

Do you remember my youthful advice about finding renewed faith in assimilating delicate dewdrops of GOD-like humility and consciously nominating your foolish sniding besting rebuttal.

CHRISTOPHER, *cowed very nepentheously, fobs-off lenient logic*

Munificent mystical mulling numbs negatively nap-like moments of nude doubt.

PHELIM, *much nooked by Christopher's nihilism, bought his glad news*

I gave good nubs of logical advice so Bernadette can't lop-off all the branches of the sensorial tree. I will always clap myself on the back for being such a friend in need!

The sound of a car engine sends Christopher hurrying into the front parlour, rushing back to the kitchen he dispatches Phelim.

CHRISTOPHER

Get going you, cause I need a few private moments to say thank-you to Bernadette.

PHELIM,
muttering
something about
certain friends
getting
preferential
treatment   O.K. – I know when I'm not wanted, I'll
                            go out but remember your uncle is due
                            back at noon.

CHRISTOPHER,
throwing a
dishcloth just
misses Phelim as
he dashes out the
back door   Get Out.

The chirpy bell rings and Christopher goes to open the door.
Bernadette dressed demurely in navy blue looks cheerful as
Christopher lonesomely admits his friend. Christopher and Ber-
nadette in their distress both attempt to speak at the same time,
then dissolve into laughter at their childish gaucheness.

CHRISTOPHER,
opening the door
of the sitting
room   Come in here Bernadette and take a seat.

BERNADETTE,
nun-like smilingly
nestles her long
legs underneath
her chair and
bravely motions
Christopher to sit   My poor annexed man more sweeter news
                            I never heard – your letter answered my
                            secret wish for you.

CHRISTOPHER,
passing cigarettes   Bernadette, will you have one?

BERNADETTE	No, I have given-up smoking for Lent – my life is hell without my fags!
CHRISTOPHER, *smoking deeply*	Can I make you a cup of coffee?
BERNADETTE *momentarily hesitates*	Yes, I'd love some coffee.
CHRISTOPHER *stands up and kindly opens the door*	Come on into the kitchen and we can chat as the milk heats.
BERNADETTE *venially moves to make the coffee*	Can I make it, looking pityful won't make the coffee taste any better!
CHRISTOPHER *hands over the jar of coffee*	Here angel of mercy, I suppose my coffee being cohesive brew, very likely it might sicken you.
BERNADETTE *lifts the milk and pours it into the coffee mugs*	Now Christopher, let's talk about your beautiful manly decision to get back between the handles of the plough and continue to till the Lord's Garden.
CHRISTOPHER, *much moved by the delicate way Bernadette described his return to the fold*	Bernadette can I say sanely but lovingly

that a brave girl's kindness and compassion
joined with candid advice bristled mighty,
needing notes fervently amening.

BERNADETTE,
*making all
benevolent
mindful genial
moves to make all
fond cautious
farewells easy for
Christopher, vests
interest in* GOD's
poor nun's calling

Christopher, now can I tell you my news
– quite often my thoughts meander to-
wards the Benedictines. Now, see why I
could not consider your beautiful senti-
ments that day on our Skelligs Rock picnic,
and had to dearly steer away from priestly
celibacy's manly virginity.

CHRISTOPHER,
*numbed by
Bernadette's news*

Let me take-in what you're saying – Ber-
nadette are you planning a nun's contem-
plative order as being where you want to
live out your days?

BERNADETTE *smilingly nods, nods, nods her head.*

CHRISTOPHER
*shouts with
laughter*

Lord, what an eejit I made of myself on
Skelligs.

BERNADETTE,
giggling too

Everyone should be allowed to call them-
selves an eejit at least once in their lifetime.

CHRISTOPHER, *moaning with pity for himself*	I will always remember the Skelligs Rock as my final humility.
BERNADETTE, *not least wanting to seem lonely, stands and picking up her handbag*	Come see me sometimes – friends should never lose touch, especially such old friends.
CHRISTOPHER *leads the way to the door*	Bernadette my dearest friend, thank you for making me see sense and thank you too for being the loveliest girl in my life.

Taking Bernadette in his arms dearly he hugs her and with tears flowing down his face he kisses fondly her tear stained cheek. Then opening the door he whispers GOD *bless you Bernadette, as she walks away.*

The cameras follow in her footsteps, then leave the scene and sweep away towards the mountains.

The End

8 February – 9 May 1980

Nolonger

Lonely, very tame, dependent,
Always wifely-old,
Poor, life-pilgrim,
Lily-sweet members
Always neat, awake
Nursed mutely, loving,
All travail,
Life a lovable niche –
Wampum-moves towards God's
Lovely Doorway to Heaven.

24 September 1979

Always?

Lovely life in all film-like green,
Always mingling timid dawnlight –
Often clinging lifelike, leaves of
Lime, glowing immaculately midst
Always Iberian lacapplied light,
Minuscule alterations in artistic
Arrangements, give a trellis
Effect to amicable poor life.

Among mulling obscure opening fossiling,
Waves of smiling memorizing loveliness
Always tip rims of trees' lumber,
Lamps lighting our secret past.
Always and ever linking our forests,
With millenniums' intrinsic intriguing illuminations,
All mighty amicable arbours in infancy,
Immortality meanwhile letters its horde.

Total a timid school's instruction,
Introduce intricate, intoxicating man,
Vivify alert intelligent language
Ratify always, rich intuitive plans.
Always open eyes towards God's immense vision,
Verily get times inherent mienful score,
Aim to immediately imbed innate tonal,
Life always dictates year's naifly abode.

I wrote the above poem for my mother on her birthday.

7 October 1979

Christmas – Lovely Ferial

Adeste Fideles flowed in the night,
Cain our baby immune by fright,
Augustus moved his writ and made declare,
Mary and Joseph and their expected Love's Care.

Naturally noble the Manchild was born,
Mother gave life alone, in Temporizing Morn,
Numberless mortizing neutralizing dreams
Were wrapped in modest, tenacious, linen seams.

Mary aved Almighty Alpha, Jesus her son,
Joseph her husband gallantly made Factual – Palmsun,
No timorous thought can mention amelioration,
Without mystically realizing God's munificent Creation.

12 November 1979

The Pet

My typewriter now is obsolete,
It's told of my tongue-tied
        genetic dreams,
Munificent mendicant hags
Spouted cestus's loincloth,
Cannot the awful poverty
           ever be minimised
           momentarily,
By a computerized friend?

19 February 1980

Timely

I got a Micro-processor,
My Mother hangs around,
She forgets that I can operate
Without her efforts now.
Nobody can imagine,
My escape route from despair,
It came from many nations,
Who read *The Times* as
Sunday prayer. The surplus
Money may provide many mighty
Mesmerizing dreams, for
Handicapped – imprisoned, isolated,
Tongue-tied, to feel welcomed
By the world – released.

The Sunday Times launched an appeal for funds to purchase a computer for
me. The appeal was a huge success. The Handicapped Children's Aid
Committee of London presented me with the complete unit. It was at this

stage that the Christopher Nolan Trust was set up, and all surplus funds
from the appeal were at my request allocated to the providing of
computerized equipment for other tongue-tied, disabled people.

9 March 1980

Five Poems

Do You?

Lunatics nearly nominated madness,
Normal nebulae broke feignedly through,
Menfolk munched on brittle traithnins,*
Nodding women snored and cauterized,
Mentioning, I don't believe it, do you?

* Traithnin - from the Gaelic - a hard withered blade of grass.

Could You?

Bernadette breathed beauty on lonely boyhood;
Nought was wanted in gloriously rendered main.
Could you imagine me, seeing and noting
Many mundane images which moved hither and thither?
In my mind, no longer normal, they became magnificent
Notions, and consequently my harried brain leaned
Downward on my chest, thinking, memorizing,
Repeating, listening in my ear for the
Effect of my words. I realized my munificence
Of knowledge. I endangered my freedom
Of expression, if I did not disembowel
My notorious madness, in impeccable
Language, agonizingly written, in numerous
Tantalizing, spasmodic-ridden onslaughts,
On a rickety, moaning typewriter.

You Could?

Newman said nobody is their brother's keeper,
Aquinas said candour in belief cannot be negative,
Centuries lovingly lustered lonely mystic's
                              mental diadems,
Ireland lengthens her benign dangerous
                              nefarious assumptions,
Could access to nullifying nemesis venially
                              mummify pentateuch,
Could easy nuggets be sampled freely, negatively,
                              newly,
Mammoth, notable, immediate vexed questions
                              bear answering,
Census point to new heady awareness in cloistered
                              irrelevancy,
Could you imagine nothing of God in the
                              wonderful future – you could?

If You?

Vellum balls benign men made,
In knowledge made benign.
Cunning men must not –
Become, bold nor benign.

Beauty cares not on whom
She falls, bother thinks
Likewise too, mental agility
Beckons at youth's
Numbest candidate too.

Nothing can chill the
Nectar neat, in bee's
Noble mead, caves-men
Noted increasingly cutely,
How marvellously lasting bees breed.

Nothing dangerous can ever fan
Celestial-breathing benignity,
Much beneficent tellings
Centuries moodily nestle with dignity.

Benedictions blew between
Sanguine men, cautioning
All of them to bear, their
Cross in beautiful certainty,
Finding ease at the well of care.

Nursing neat awareness
Unlikely before, all eager
Took hope intow, and vanquished
And loser voced love's delights,
And voiced caution no more.

Nought were the nemesis –
Centuries cascaded on,
Another day had dawned,
Seeming weakly in despair
Calming influence lingered there.

Bending certainty endemically,
Bestial address melted through,
Bold enterprise bonded meekly –
Null and mournful, battening menfolk
Announced, "I, Rabbi, if You let me,
Will sweetly feel as You?"

The above poem contains my personal philosophy, "Always lean on Christ for support."

Try?

Christ's news came neatly-
Packed, in beautiful vales

Of tears, melting snow-white
Bends in the verdant, nigh
Azure-blue vaults of the
Firmament, freeing numerous,
Countless samples of benign
Faith in God's cool, clear
Waters of sweet, sparkling,
Clam-like, death-defying
Sustenance, succulently supplied –
In heady delightful, denim-lasting
Franchise, upon the Altar of Love.
Nolonger could cedars credo
Asleep, nolonger could numbness –
In feelings be heard, nobody
Feared all mesmeric doubt,
None but sullen fools
Castigated canon nought,
Veritable vineyards of novel
New prayer, opened chasms
As deep as Middle Eastern
Oil's layer, luminating
Centuries' veins buried deep,
Certifying clearly noble
Nicene's brave creed, calming
Christians' tired trying and
Nullifying fear, making
Insistent invitations, to
Try bearing near – Try?

7–8 April 1980

Naturally

Children helping vestal memories,
Numbing nature's nude semesters,
Centuries carrying children's nerves,
Anointing nectar-sweet nuggets,
Cabling beauteous ventures amulets
Among needs as deep as oceans,
Wetting certain centre codes,
Mending nesting-bird gaiety,
Fecunding pampered world wealth,
Nominating nourishing beads-poor,
Mentioning memorabilia in abundance,
Navigating-nigh man's nothingness.

Munificent beneficent blessings bleed
Nappy-lined with lively love,
Bludgeoning mulling-life's cancer,
Mummifying crematoriumly look's genes,
Malleabling verdures childish dreams,
Netting notorious nets mundaneness,
Moulding breathing beauty's benignity,
Cresting celestial genetic gentleness,
Festooning freedom's dallient endeavours,
Caballing caustically candid caring
Nannying negotiations, naturally, normally
Nestling, within cheerful children.

15 May 1980

Lovely Months

January

Numb snow mush on noon-tide line,
Nought neat now, for day wears on,
Altering a white-mantled poor land,
Changing moribund mourning to numbness.

February

Cometh cement coloured clouds, cental-
Carrying beneficent, commending, caressing care,
Cunningly ceiling celestial, cabling ceding,
Compelling cancerous malignancy –
Maniacally breathing coquettish, calming centuries-
Certitude, verruculently mucusing nouveau-year's
Camaraderie, caballing vanity's nucleus-heaped
Cancellations, in magic intriguing customary
Manifold vraiments, of belligerent nature's noblesse noblige.

March

Been careful to need clothes, mulling-
Cold, calling clock-late, crowingly
Castle-clowning endless life,
Cooking curry-hot clanging
Meals, bleeding-clothed clock-
Cost, memorizing March month.

April

Queerly clinging life-loving machine,
Playing calm man's movable acts,
Clinch, clean, clang moccassing,
Notable in cones casting nets new-
Seals upon neatness-locked notation,
Cementing nebulae verdantly, elevating
All lunatic-dappled land,
Negating muscles co-ordination,
Lining apron's nonchalance likewise,
Aping fallows-lonely, God-gifted cloy,
Classed mammy-dallied appointed April-Fool.

May

And innately, nothing, nobody –
Yearning nightly, praying nightly,
Although cutting margins, inroads
Constant, cobra-coiled, constrained,
Cheerfully negotiating normal nut-brown
Avenues, meekly, cutely, cementing-
Patience, neck-tied callously,
Centuries-embeddedly, naturally-neatly,
Succeedingly tightly around graciously-
Comforting, May month's beautiful mothers.

June

Bountiful valleys nourishing non-bugling horns,
Scenting mundane mental mangles, breaking evenly
Numb-nevers, nude-nothings, needs-nuisance,
Needle-notches, clanish-canters customarily
Neutral-nonage, needing care, courage and
Combined June month's wedding-day promise.

July

Benedictions cannot befriend cases,
Life calls the cards, cowards lose-
Out, deeds nominate numerous knights,
Beating naughty moots mutations,
Beckoning neatly-notched, candidly-
Coated candles to light the dark, cancerous-
Corridors of cloudy July's pregnant-promises.

August

Nothing mummifyingly nominates mysteries –
Schooling lets merit spring-step straight
Towards seeming brilliant careers, mastering
Centuries non-ligamented, muchly-longed lease,
Changing much cental, cubbyholed secrets,
Cementing cesural, venial-like intimidations,
Nesting central cesspool-hopes neglect,
Genetically gesticulating dossier's looks,
Clenching cellulose, numbing, beautifying-
Credentials, clustered in coiling, clinging-
People's poor licence, decreeing candidly-
Calm, all isolated, humble, humid, luminous, central
Certain August, Lental month's acquittal.

September

Nestling clown-cake life –
Lonely nebulae ceaseless –
Cleansing claustrophobic-
Numbness, nursing necklaces –
Focusing offers of efflorescent-
September voxes, cheering –
Exciting, boy-carefree
Cubbyholes of joie-de-vivre.

October

Beautifully mellow, oven-like nuts, cooked
Brown-ripe all summer long, centuries-
Coined, small kernel-assimilations,
Cement-hard shells cream-tipping life,
Always cementing veal-tender dreams –
Peacefully encased within October's
Autumnal, closeted, cloistered granary.

November

Always, cells cede defatigable defeat,
Cunningly letting-on that cruel-
Nature, invisibly caballed with –
Devious, blunt, never-no-more,
In meting-out murderous
Cold degrading death –
To foggy November's
Traithnin treasa.*

December

Mouthing moidered monologues,
Clutching bulbous mundaneness,
Man's imminent boldness –
Festered and fumed, vehement
In cubbyholing all meritorious-
Mention, opulently suggesting
Comfit, camcoiled lonesomely
Around zany, bonny December.

20 May 1980

---

* Traithnin treasa – the Gaelic description of hoar-frost – pronounced
trawneen trassa.

Annihilation

Needful, needless, needs,
Intellectually non-starters,
Yelling foolish fears –
Isolated, dead, cells.

10 July 1980

Tempting

Now that momentary-heady quietness
Cements my melancholic dreams,
Certifying saving Phil's* great aid,
Sealing cursing, neurotic answers –
Mesmerizing vender's astute provisions,
Celestial cemeteries give-up souls
Hitherto polarized in hellish torments,
Meandering memories edge me forward,
Bullying my evaporating spasm's credence,
Meaning, gearing, even driving –
Piercing, creature-conning comfort,
In endless, meek-man's Magnanimous Dream.†

14 July 1980

---

* Phil Odor, the computer expert who devised special programmes which
enabled me to operate on my own and thereby write without my mother's
assistance, although total independence in composition is still several years
away.
† My secret dream, in which I see countless disabled, speechless people being
helped through the use of technology to find expression for their once
imprisoned thoughts.

158, Vernon Avenue,
Clontarf, Dublin 3.
18th July 1980

Dear Phil,

Let me say feebly how very grateful I am to you and to all my host of friends in Edinburgh University. Be happy in the assurance that poor tokens of gratitude just cannot hope to convey my candid, voluminous, numbifying, boyish disbelief that there could exist a man such as you.

No doubt you are wondering how my chin-switch is progressing, I put great new moiety-backed hope in it.

We are going to take a much needed break in August, believe me Phil, I need it badly.

May I mention again – my chinswitch mummifyingly moulds my lonely lost despair.

Could you imagine my happy hack memorably, benignly mentioning new moist-eyed happy love?

Your friend,
Christy.

And Now?

Certain lonely peals,
Cemetery-fopped noise,
Mulling centennial volts,
Mouthing mumbled mention,
Clenching mental tears,
Clearly misunderstood.

And now, magnetism
Members my verbosity,
Nudging nude belles-lettres,
Weaving mundane logic
Into mercurial dreams.

23 July 1980

Cannot

Such nocts between,
Moonlight nudges
Jostling nocturnal numbness
Into nomadic depths,
Cellulose mundane clouds
Nostalgically enfold
Mental meandering musing,
Nibbling beads of
Knowledge, nolonger netting
Balmy benediction,
In lonesome blacknight
Sleepless sighing silence.

25 July 1980

Kindest Tact

Much meaning mentally noted,
Ventilating mundane word's sphere,
Cementing beautiful, banana-like creations,
Outprising lonesome, lemon-sour dreams.

28 August 1980

Class

Clever children cited –
Camera-loaded for show,
Class-scoffed, neurotic-cloned, life's-
Outcasts, left neglected, alone.

28 August 1980

Chagrin

Cemetery-closetted grandparents,
Lightly-slumbering, close,
Aged sentinels, sampling
Death's éclat.

28 August 1980

Cemetery

Candid, manmade crosses
Love's lively evidence,
Nestling a much beloved couple,
Interred nobly, screened, spent.

28 August 1980

Numbing God

Boldly delightful,
Speaking real slow,
Nudging me onwards –
Calling insistently – "Christy".

28 August 1980

Nominating

Pity the man in failure,
Love the man who's mad,
Make music with the man that's happy,
Marvel at a lonesome-child's hand;
Outstretched in those innocent fingers
Is a lively benediction's grace,
Make careful study, make mercy chime,
Love the tear, dry the face, watch the smile.

28 August 1980

Life

Conceived, land-locked,
Amending men, love-choked,
Clenching teeth, newly
Nashing in murderous,
Cumbersome, lead-laden,
Loitering labour.

28 August 1980

Clonbonny

Nomadic memories call me back,
Alarming natural credibility,
Molten nebulae nurturing –
A pipe with tobacco smell,
A man with candid gaze,
A lovely mantelpiece;
A beautiful wedding picture –
All caved with bright lustrous peace;
A lively conversation,
Everywhere spic and span,
A home for every generation –
Even a grandson.

28 August 1980

Ongoing

Feeling beastly-nasty,
Many discuss me so –
Can he hear? Can he see?,
Can fools fly? Evidently no!

28 August 1980

Noble Company

Amiable companions,
Bonnie girl's talk –
Breathes mink-coated
Loveliness, in my
Drab-dreamed world.

My poem 'Noble Company' sums up my feelings as I live-out each school-
day among my lovely friends in Class 3L, Mount Temple.

28 August 1980

Imprints

Henceforth, men moodily cement –
Vivid beautiful memories,
Penpoised accrued entries,
Neatly noted in dimwitted-appearing
Amounts, snowscaped from ice-creams
Of wafer-packed loves-delights,
And gently cemented into clear clods
Of cental-packed penchant,
Amorous, non-plussed, vehement
Naturalness, which lasts a manly lifetime.

30 August 1980

Bells, Now Cheerfully

Ponder, cities, always man's brag,
Coldly number cathedrals bare,
Account for man's cunning
Playing games, seeing naught
Laying begged, cemeteries carrion?

2 September 1980

Nolan

Answers come to all cameod puzzles,
Moving everyone dole-asteriskally,
Letting-on that life, man-loathed,
Gets easier, just because bemiring met me.

The above poem is dedicated to my family.

2 September 1980

Crabs

Momentary mention of crabs,
Newly musters maritime-
Nature's bragging tantrums,
Mountainous seas, hordes of
Hidden-depths' livers,
Dumped molestingly upon
The sick strand.

3 September 1980

Cemented

Nemesis may maces carve, acceding
Man's brute-strength, nailing bombs –
Hampered blitzing, coldly crushing
Ceding cruel cobalt carnage, to careless
Coverting, caballing, conniving noct.

3 September 1980

Lady Goulding

Slowly, slowly, slowly,
Love wishes as love does,
Pealing bragging bells of faith
In the sobbing place of woe
Fostering lovely hope, asleep,
Offended and heart-worn,
Giving measle-spotted help
To a handicapped-man forlorn,
Castigating gospel stories
Of Samaritan special help,
She diligently sought an answer
Kathleen* found time, told well;
Capitalizing on caring people
Offering monetary help, twixt
Love and serene suffering,
They built a bridge to health,
Now, celestial glory 'waits them,
Graciously foretold, by One who
Raised the crippled-man, Divinely,
In Capernaum – so long ago.

3 September 1980

*Kathleen O'Rourke: co-founder of The C.R.C.

Members

Cares leave man mean,
Birth cleaves, life's-marked
Mundane babble's cellulosing,
Attires mesmerising dreams,
Brinking beads of banking
Clouded consciousness, revealing
A scarlet-dabbed canvas,
Cratered fissures mingling
War's vascular haemorrhage.

5 September 1980

Dastardly

Pushed, nulled, bossed,
Sampled, cowed, conned,
Benedictions cover everything;
Banishing the numbness,
Ceding the vendetta,
Cosseting the dastardly,
Serving the masochistic
Casts chemise-cosy balm
Acceding éclat's aisance.*

5 September 1980

* aisance – from the French, meaning easiness of life.

Haematin

Let's look at bleeding-man's wounded,
Lift off each divergent skin,
Nolonger note birth's life-looks,
Rather, identify characterizing haematin.

2 September 1980

Munificence

Count man, boldly braving life,
Clutching medieval know-how,
Doing credit to Camelot.

2 September 1980